Kenneth A Behr

ROAMING CATHOLICS

Ending the wandering
to embrace the wonder

ISBN-13: 978-1-63452-792-7
Library of Congress Control Number: 2014921011

Xpyria Press
Palm Beach Gardens, FL 33418
Printed in the United States of America

For further information regarding this topic or to connect with the author contact Xpyria Press through the website: Xpyria.org

To my friends, my family, and all of those that have encouraged this effort. In particular to my wife, who has challenged me to be a better disciple of Jesus Christ, which makes me a better friend, husband, father, and grandfather.

Contents

Contents

Preface

Since the very beginning, we have tried to divide what Jesus said should be one. In his Gospel, John recorded Jesus's prayer in the Garden of Gethsemane. Here is how Jesus prayed for us just hours before His arrest and His going to the cross:

> My prayer is not for them alone. I pray also for those who will believe in me through their message that all of them may be one, Father, just as you are in me and I am in you. May they also be in us so that the world may believe that you have sent me. I have given them the glory that you gave me, that they may be one as we are one—I in them and you in me—so that they may be brought to complete unity. Then the world will know that you sent me and have loved them even as you have loved me. (John 17:20–23)

Jesus prayed that we would be one or, in other words, united. Unity, or being one, is actually a big topic in the New Testament. Jesus prayed for it three times; the apostle Paul spoke about it often.

For years I have met people who still considered themselves spiritual, still believed in something, but were either no longer attending Mass or worship service or were not involved with other people on the basis of their faith.

The largest group of Christians in the United States is Roman Catholic. According to the Pew Research Center, approximately 31 percent of Americans, or one in three, were raised as Roman Catholic. However, Pew Research also found that one third of all people raised Roman Catholic no longer consider themselves Catholic,[1] meaning that approximately 10 percent of all Americans are former Catholics, many of them still wandering without finding another church home or returning to the Catholic Church.

This is unfortunate and a failure of the institution part of the church. All too often we have embraced our denominations, our cultures, and our traditions and mistakenly thought these were the basis of our faith.

We should not ground our faith in our denominations, our traditions, or our culture but in the life, death, and resurrection of Jesus Christ. It was early in the development of the church that we saw these schisms, divisions, and dissensions beginning to form. The apostle Paul, writing from Ephesus, a city in present-day Turkey, around AD 55 or 56, addressed the "jealousy and quarreling" (1 Cor. 3:3) in the church in Corinth:

> For when one says, "I follow Paul," and another, "I follow Apollos," are you not mere human beings? What, after all, is Apollos? And what is Paul? Only servants, through whom you came to believe—as the Lord has assigned to each his task. I planted the seed, Apollos watered it, but God has been making it grow. (1 Cor. 3:4–6)

I believe it's not coincidental that one of these early disputes was about the human leaders. Church leaders are never perfect; the only one who ever lived a perfect life was Jesus Christ.

The early apostles were imperfect both before and after Pentecost, when the Holy Spirit came to dwell in their mortal bodies. Jesus had to rebuke the apostles a number of times over His three years with them. New Testament author Luke told the story in the ninth chapter of his Gospel of an argument among the apostles about which of them would be the greatest. A little later, while entering a Samaritan town, the apostles asked Jesus if they should "call fire down from heaven to destroy them [the village]." Jesus rebuked them.

The apostle Peter, of course, is an easy target if we are looking for an apostle who seemed imperfect. People who are quick to judge Peter are often far from perfect themselves. Peter was a great leader, but he was rash, quick to judge, and too confident in his flesh. Peter denied Christ three times; however, Christ restored him.

A few years later, the apostle Paul met the apostle Peter in Antioch and had to call him a hypocrite:

> When Cephas came to Antioch, I opposed him to his face, because he stood condemned. For before certain men came from James, he used to eat with the Gentiles. But when they arrived, he began to draw back and separate himself from the Gentiles because he was afraid of those who belonged to the circumcision group. The other Jews joined him in his hypocrisy, so that by their hypocrisy even Barnabas was led astray. (Gal. 2:11–13)

Paul was not trying to cause a division in the church. Note that Paul didn't talk about Cephas (Peter) behind his back but "opposed him to his face." Paul directed his discipline not only at Peter but also to those who continued to think of the world as consisting of two contrasting groups: Jews or Gentiles. This Jewish thinking was similar to the Greek thinking of "Greek or Barbarian" or even today's "Catholic or Protestant."

The apostle Paul referred to the church as the "Body of Christ." Not once did he refer to it as the "Body of Christians." He taught that there was no longer Jew or Greek, slave or free, male or female, but all were one in Christ.[2]

The world needs the real Jesus. All too often religion masks the real Jesus in customs, traditions, and bureaucratic institutions that care more about the perpetuation of their own organizations than advancing the good news of the Gospel and making disciples of Jesus.

There has been one church for more than two thousand years. The church is the Body of Christ; it is not an institution. When Jesus told Peter He would "build His church," He was referring to a people, not a denomination. The word translated, church, comes from the Greek term *ekklesia*—"upon this Rock I will build my *ekklesia*" (Matt. 16:18)—which is formed from two Greek words meaning "an assembly" and "to call out" or "called-out ones." To summarize Jesus's teaching in Matthew 16:18, the New Testament Church is a body of believers whom God has called out from the world to live as His people under the authority of Jesus Christ.

Interestingly the present English word church is most closely related to the German word *kirche*, which was a religious building used by pagans. As Christians embraced the word and it assimilated into English, people often thought of the church as a building.

My Story

Once a Catholic, Always a Catholic

Hell, as illustrated in *Hortus Deliciarum*, a twelfth-century work by a French nun. Photographic reproduction and original work in the public domain.

Perhaps you have heard this: "You have fallen away!" Or perhaps, "What are we going to tell the family?" These are the comments people hear when they are no longer attending the Catholic Church. People who grew up Catholic and stopped attending can attest that the saying "once a Catholic, always a Catholic" has been likely used and probably abused.

For a time in my life, I heard those words. I was brought up in a Catholic family and educated in a Catholic school, and I embraced Catholicism as an adult. However, soon after we were married and had our children, my wife and I started attending a non-denominational church. My mom and dad as well as many in my family questioned our newfound faith and the reason why we were seemingly abandoning our religion.

One day when I was traveling through Indiana for business, I took the opportunity to visit my favorite aunt and uncle. The conversation over dinner quickly turned to religion. It was a good conversation, and I gave them all of the reasons why we felt it was important for us to attend a great church in our neighborhood.

My aunt turned to me and said, "Once a Catholic, always a Catholic." It was not a statement of reason but an emotional appeal she was making to her nephew. She knew only the Catholic Church and believed it to be the one and only true church.

From my perspective my wife and I hadn't converted or abandoned anything; we were actually embracing our faith and growing closer to God. To us, moving from one location on Sunday to another wasn't about converting to another faith but reaffirming what we knew to be true.

Our journey as Catholics had started with baptisms as infants decades earlier. However, our deep and personal relationships with Jesus Christ in reality had started during a ninety-day period, from Ash Wednesday to Pentecost Sunday, just a few years prior. It began when our Catholic priest, whom we had gotten to know, invited us to a Catholic charismatic group meeting on Tuesdays starting the first full week of Lent. We had asked a few questions about getting to know some other couples and growing in our faith. He told us about this little group and said there was a break at Easter, so if we didn't feel the group was for us we could easily just drop out.

We didn't drop out, and because of this group of committed, charismatic Catholics as well as a number of other things that seemed to be calling us to more, God changed our lives during those ninety days. We purchased our first Bible and started reading it on a daily basis. After the ninety days, we found a similar and even larger group that met on Fridays in a gym and occasionally in a park. We enjoyed the fellowship and the scripture reading. Someone always had a guitar, and we learned new songs and began to experience worship in a new and meaningful way. We loved meeting and getting to know other Christians who were as excited about their faith as we were.

The Friday group included young and old, married couples, singles, and a few younger children. For the first time, we heard about having a personal relationship with Jesus. We knew what that was and could look back to that ninety-day period and feel how much our hearts had changed. The language we were using about our faith was also changing. It wasn't as much going to Mass as it was being in fellowship with other believers. The group was primarily Catholics, but they referred more and more to themselves as believers or spirit filled and even born again. We found we had everything in common with these people as well as other Christians who read the Bible for wisdom, devotions, and personal growth and desired to have living relationships with Jesus Christ.

That was in the early 1980s, and the charismatic renewal of the Catholic Church was in full swing. It seems like every family had one of *those* kinds. In our family it was my wife and I. We were the ones who seemed always to find a way to turn any conversation into a conversation about Jesus. It seemed like our favorite activities were reading our Bibles and listening to Christian radio and Christian music. Our kids were still very young, and we wanted the very best for them. We started looking for a church that could help us grow, that would be a great place for our young children to learn about God, and that would give us an opportunity to meet other couples who were just as passionate about their relationships with God as we were.

In the beginning I had more passion and enthusiasm than common sense. I was insensitive, rude, argumentative, and no fun to have at a party. My wife was much more pleasant. She didn't like arguments and was a natural peacemaker. In time God was able to smooth out some of these rough edges in my life, and my family eventually forgave me. Surprisingly, and over time, they started to see, through my gentler and humbler self, that my faith in and love for God were real. I've found this approach to be better when we want to share the Gospel. St. Francis of Assisi once said, "Preach the Gospel at all times, and if necessary use words."[3]

Over the years I've had the opportunity to read and grow and have taken some classes in theology, the Bible, and history. I've learned a lot about my Catholic heritage. Had I known then what I know now, I would have had better answers to people who asked about me falling away or abandoning my religion. To me Catholicism was a great inheritance, and it was in the Catholic Church that I came to believe the essential truths I continue to believe today. The faith, the history, the traditions, and even the doctrines contributed greatly to who I am.

I am writing this book because of these experiences. I am much more than a former Catholic. I have an appreciation of my Catholic heritage, the Catholic members of my family, and all of the wonderful members of the Body of Christ who attend Catholic churches. This is my story, but I will also be sharing the story of the church through history, which influenced my thinking and clarified my thoughts. The history of the church will include the dates and the people and the places, but it will also be the story, the narrative of how the church has evolved. My evolution, however, began more than forty years ago, when I was still in Catholic school.

CHAPTER ONE

Catholic School

The Catholics and the Publics

Dominican nuns arriving at St. Joseph's School in the early
1960s. Photograph in the public domain.

I was in the third grade at St. Joseph's Catholic School when one of my friends, Randy Dirks, became a Cub Scout. Pack 324 set up shop in the basement (which was also our third-grade classroom) at St. Joseph's, and soon many of the kids in my class were attending meetings monthly. One of our neighbors, Mrs. Zins, the mother of two sons the same age as my brother and I, became a den leader, with weekly Bear Cub pack meetings at her house.

For some reason I wasn't initially attracted to the thought of hanging out with the boys in my class at Cub Scout meetings. Perhaps it was because I couldn't see the value in swapping my Catholic school uniform, consisting of a blue shirt, blue pants, and a blue crisscross tie, for the Cub Scout blue shirt, blue pants, and yellow neckerchief. However, over time, and particularly when I heard something about a pinewood derby, it became more intriguing.

One of my closest friends was Dennis Semro. He lived around the corner and went to a public school, not to St. Joseph's. I didn't know much about religion at the time. I focused my mind on watching *Superman* on TV and playing baseball. I was really disappointed that Dennis wouldn't and couldn't join Pack 324 with me. He and his brothers and sisters were "publics," and the publics had their own Cub Scout pack. The one that met at St. Joseph's was only for the Catholics.

While Dennis and I were best friends, we went to different schools and different churches. His was Lutheran. Dennis was the first person who ever invited me to his church. One summer, around the same year, he invited me to his church's vacation Bible school, or VBS. It sounded like fun and promised to be a week of summer activities culminating with an ice-cream social that parents could attend as well. I brought the flyer Dennis gave me to my mom. However, she and Dad didn't even consider the VBS idea and dismissed my request. They told me we were Catholics, and we couldn't attend events at Lutheran churches.

In many families, people believe they can't attend events at churches other than their own denominations. The Roman Catholic Church formalized this idea a number of times over the years, including in the St. Joseph Baltimore Catechism, which was first published in 1885.

The Catholics were not the first to put together a catechism. The lack of religious instruction that both the clergy and laity had dismayed Martin Luther, and he published Luther's Large Catechism in 1529.[4] The Roman Catholic Church was slow to respond to Luther. After the Council of Trent, however, there was a renewed emphasis on education, particularly for the clergy. While early Catholic catechisms going back to the seventeenth century were for the clergy to read, not the laity, the Baltimore Catechism had an edition just for students.

My first Baltimore Catechism was probably a condensed version for elementary students. I remember it was green, and I kept it in my desk at school. It was likely an updated version of the original, but it still seemed old even back in the 1960s. The Baltimore Catechism consisted of lessons, a few prayers to memorize, and a number of questions.

The original catechism is now in the public domain, so I was able to find a couple of the questions and answers that dealt with this issue of visiting other churches, including joining a Cub Scout pack.

Q 205. How does a Catholic sin against faith?

A. A Catholic sins against faith by apostasy, heresy, indifferentism, and by taking part in non-Catholic worship.

Q 206. Why does a Catholic sin against faith by taking part in non-Catholic worship?

A. A Catholic sins against faith by taking part in non-Catholic worship when he intends to identify himself with a religion he knows is defective.

For hundreds of years, both Catholics and Protestants have taught that it is sinful, harmful, and dangerous to get too close to each other. This is so unfortunate, as there is so much we can learn from each other. The Bible clearly tells us there is only one church, with Jesus as the head. In the Gospel of John, Jesus prayed for unity. He was praying for His disciples, but He included all of us:

3

Neither pray I for these alone, but for them also which shall believe on me through their word; That they all may be one; as you, Father, are in me, and I in you, that they also may be one in us: that the world may believe that you have sent me. And the glory, which you gave me, I have given them; that they may be one, even as we are one. (John 17:20–21, NASB)

Many can relate to this struggle between Catholics and Protestants. Religious persecution is no laughing matter, as the Thirty Years' War (1618–1648) devastated much of Europe, and Germany lost literally one half of all of its young men in battles and the resulting pestilence and disease. This was not a war against barbarian pagans but with Christians drawing swords against other Christians. These were nations and kingdoms and cities led by kings who believed in God, understood the Trinity, embraced the death and resurrection of Jesus Christ for their sins as an historical fact, yet found it appropriate to wage war against others who believed the same.

CHAPTER TWO

Early Persecution and the Martyrs

Sticks and Stones May Break My Bones

Icon of the martyrdom of St. Ignatius of Antioch.
Photographic reproduction and original work in the
public domain.

Whenyou think about it, the old idiom "sticks and stones may break my bones, but words will never hurt me" is just dumb. Today we understand how harmful words can be. Recently CBS did a special called "Bullying: Words Can Kill."[5] Even as a child, I knew that words can and do hurt. Children find this out very quickly when they experience and often join in on name calling. Simple and complete nonsense words such as *Dumbo, Dopey,* and *brainiac* can cause embarrassment and a feeling of being an outcast. Children learn the stylistic and memorable quality of consonance early, and I've noticed with my children and now my grandchildren that names such as Fat Freddy, Smelly Sally, and Nerdy Nelly never seem to go out of style.

I was in third or fourth grade at St. Joseph's Catholic School when a small group of us decided to form our own informal club. Some of the older boys in some of the upper grades had started a Secret Agent Club. Sean Connery starred as James Bond in the 1965 theatrical release of *Goldfinger.* Our mothers wouldn't allow us to see it. The Catholic Church had a posted list of movies that were OK and those we were to avoid. Their ratings, from A to L and O (for offensive), preceded by decades today's ratings of G, PG, PG-13, and R and carried a lot of weight with Hollywood in general and my mom in particular. Since we couldn't see the movie and the older boys didn't want us in their club, we decided to start our own.

My friends and I all enjoyed comic books, so we started a club that was all about them. We would buy DC and Marvel comics for only twelve cents. However, the price soon changed to fifteen cents, and a double issue was easily a quarter. My friend Mike Baron came up with the idea, and about half of the boys in Sister Annunciata's class were part of our club, which we ended up calling the Legion, short for the Legion of Super Heroes. Each of us had our favorite hero or villain. In reality it was a comic book exchange club, but to us it felt like something heroic.

My favorite was always Superman, and I wasn't that particular about whether he was the younger Superboy or Superman, or whether he was the Clark Kent of Smallville or Metropolis. He could fly and bend steel with his bare hands; bullets bounced off of him, and he was my hero.

I think all of us love heroes, as they have a way of encouraging us to do things we normally wouldn't do. When it comes to real-life heroes, someone very wise once said, "Heroes are not extraordinary people but ordinary people doing extraordinary things."

In the early church, God called a group of ordinary people to do extraordinary things; we call them martyrs. The word *martyr* comes from the Greek word *mártys* and originally just meant "witness." However, when these early converts to Christianity found themselves with the choice between recanting their faith and denying Jesus Christ or remaining faithful, they remained faithful. This was a life-and-death decision. Even the historical accounts are hard to read, as the martyrs often faced death in the Roman Colosseum as morbid entertainment for the masses. The more fortunate were killed by ax or sword, but many, perhaps thousands, were lit on fire as human torches by Emperor Nero, whose use of many Christians in this manner to give light in the evenings in Rome is very well documented.

The Bible records that the believers were first called Christians in Antioch, in modern-day Turkey (Acts 11:26). One of the first bishops and early fathers of the church was St. Ignatius of Antioch. He was a disciple of John the apostle, and the emperor Trajan martyred him in Rome.

The persecution of the early church and the resulting martyrdoms of hundreds of thousands of Christian witnesses started under Roman Emperor Nero (AD 64–68) and, according to tradition, included both the apostles Peter and Paul during Nero's reign. Initially Rome considered Christianity a sect of Judaism and for years had given the Jews a special exemption to believe and worship as they pleased. This Jewish exemption was not unique, as the Roman Empire actually had been fairly tolerant of various religions as Rome spread its rule across Europe, into Asia and Northern Africa.

These Christian witnesses of the first and second centuries, however, were different. They seemed deliberately hostile toward the gods of the Roman Empire and the sacrifices that were the obligation of all Roman citizens. Ultimately they refused to participate in the offerings to the Roman gods. As a result Romans accused Christians of being athe-ists. These early Christians called their weekly gatherings "pure sacri-fices" as opposed to "offerings to demons," as they characterized the religion of the pagans. Persecution broke out for a number of reasons against the Christians and lasted for three hundred years, until Emperor Constantine claimed Christianity as his religion, which ended Christian persecution.

It's important to note that these early witnesses, these martyrs or early Christian saints, were members of the Body of Christ but were likely unfamiliar with the terms we use today to describe the church. Along with the word, Christian, which was first used of the believers in Antioch,[6] some of the other and more common words to describe early believers in Jesus included the Way and the Nazarenes.

This early group of believers was a mixed group. History tells us many were Jews and Jewish converts who embraced Jesus as the long-awaited Messiah. Their theology was still developing. Often it included a combi-nation of Jewish traditions and rabbinical teachings combined with early Christian letters. These were the words of Jesus and the writings of the apostles Peter, James, John, and Matthew, as well as the other collections that would become the New Testament. Their gatherings and worship services were varied and diverse, without a formal liturgy or established leadership structure. They believed they would see the return of Jesus Christ in their lifetime. They were willing to make extreme sacrifices for their faith, believing that Jesus would soon be coming.

CHAPTER THREE

Why History?

**Geography Has Made Us Neighbors.
History Has Made Us Friends.**
—John F. Kennedy

Posthumous official portrait of President John F. Kennedy.
Photographic reproduction and original work in
the public domain.

As a pastor it's not unusual for people to ask me theological and religious questions, such as: "Where did the Bible come from?" "Why doesn't God answer my prayer?" "Why do we attend church on Sunday rather than Saturday?"

Some of these questions are a little easier to answer than others. The questions I love to hear are the ones that afford me the opportunity to share a little history, particularly church history.

I've always been a fan of history. One of the reasons can be attributed to Mr. Everhart, a teacher I had back in high school. I was turning fourteen, and my parents had moved to a new suburb that had a brand new public high school. I had graduated from St. Joseph's grade school, and my eighth-grade class had been much like my other grades, as we had one teacher who taught all of the subjects. The only difference was that the principal, Sister Mary Ann, had decided to separate the boys from the girls so we could focus on studies rather than on girls. I graduated with thirty-five boys, and my parents hoped and prayed to St. Anthony (the patron saint of lost causes) that I was ready for high school.

My freshman year at Hillcrest High School was a culture shock from St. Joseph's. Hillcrest was brand new and a large campus in a multiethnic and multiracial suburb. In the very first week, I met Mr. Everhart, who taught a ninth-grade world history class. Mr. Everhart had a way of making history seem relevant, exciting, and fun. He taught from the unique perspective of showing us how history changed history. Battles were fought, discoveries were made, and elections were won or lost, and they changed history.

Because he was a great teacher, I became a better student. I paid attention, was a little more respectful, and caused far less trouble in his class than in other classes. However, there was one incident when I stuck a pencil in the take-up reel on a movie projector. The reel stopped, but the momentum kept the other wheel turning, and the film shot out like a bullet, hitting the front wall and blackboard fifteen feet away and spilling onto the floor.

In spite of the distractions of my youth, Mr. Everhart's teachings have stayed with me. I remember him saying, "Imagine what would have happened if the Confederate army had won the Battle of Vicksburg in July of 1864, Ulysses S. Grant had been defeated, and the Republic remained divided. How would history have been changed if the pilgrims never sailed to the New World in a ship called the *Mayflower*?"

In Mr. Everhart's history class, we talked about the recent and tragic assassination of Dr. Martin Luther King Jr. Mr. Everhart was guiding us through how this great man would be remembered as well as how his death would change the world. Just a few months later, while we were on summer break, we would hear about the assassination of Senator Robert F. Kennedy. History certainly changes history.

History is full of decisions, movements, and great men and women. We have acknowledged and recorded some of these important decisions, patriotic movements, political statesmen (both the greats and near greats), but many continue to be hidden in the pages of our history books, waiting to be discovered.

After high school I went to a private, non-Catholic college on an athletic scholarship and ended up meeting my wife. She was the prettiest girl in school, and I married her just months after graduating.

Like most newly married couples, we focused on our careers, buying our first house, and spending time with our friends. We gave little thought to church, as we were only casual attendees with very limited interest in growing our faith in God or examining our core religious beliefs.

Everything changed when we had two new babies, and we realized it was time to grow up, join a local church, and leave some semblance of a religious legacy to our children. While that sounds reasonable and straightforward to most people, remember the influence of my favorite teacher, Mr. Everhart, and his fondness for history. Our search for a good church inevitably led me to look into the history of some of the religious traditions that everyone else took for granted.

Over time, and through hours spent poring over books on religious history, I developed a passion for the history of the church. The more I read about it, the more I could see how indeed history had changed history. I had grown up thinking on Sundays and holy days I was attending a church that hadn't changed much in more than two thousand years. I really didn't understand from where some of the Catholic traditions and customs had come. Like many others I had assumed Jesus or the apostles gave them to us directly, and someone must have recorded them somewhere. Hopefully Peter or one of the other apostles took notes during his time with Jesus, walking the dusty roads of Galilee.

What I found was even more relevant and exciting. For those who share my enjoyment of history, I'll even add the word fun! The church had changed; it had adapted and grown. It had been abused, challenged, and ridiculed but had responded with resilience, patience, and relevance.

In its darkest hour, it continued to be the church. It was and continues to be the guardian of the greatest document in human history: the Bible. In the pages of the Bible, we find history and dogma, triumph and tragedy, comfort and warnings. The Bible declares itself the living Word of God; the writer of Hebrews said it is "alive and powerful. It is sharper than the sharpest two-edged sword, cutting between soul and spirit, between joint and marrow. It exposes our innermost thoughts and desires."[7] This search through the Bible and for the history of the church changed my life.

In the pages of the Bible, we find the beginnings of the church, the local and unique expression of the Body of Jesus Christ. In this beginning of the church, we see how history changed history.

From a very humble beginning with twelve apostles, including one who would betray Him, Jesus brought a teaching that was the fulfillment of thousands of years of history and prophecy. Jesus brought a new voice—one with authority, love, clarity, and hope. The rest, as they say, is history, or His story. Just a little bit of investigation opens pages of a documented history of the church that is fascinating, revealing, and even compelling.

We often think of the church as Western, dominating the culture of Europe since the time of the Caesars and the Americas since the sixteenth century. However, most people are not aware that the church started in the East, not the West. After Pentecost the church grew rapidly, but soon there were many more churches and Christians in Asia and Africa than there were in Europe. Of the original five patriarchs or leaders of the early church (we'll get into that in the next chapter), only one was in the West, in Rome; the others were located in Alexandria, Jerusalem, Antioch, and Constantinople.

The church is now becoming more Southern than Northern, as European Christianity is in decline and Christianity is growing quickly in Latin America, Africa, and Asia. The news media, including TV, radio, and the twenty-four-hour news cycle, are very quick to remind us of the demise of Christianity. To them historical Christianity has become irrelevant. They can't understand why the Roman Catholic pope doesn't just come out in favor of every imaginable vice and sin. They love telling the stories of abuse in the Catholic Church or the desperate shortage of priests and the closing of Catholic schools.

This group of liberal media elites will tell you that not only are the Catholics irrelevant; Protestants are as well. They paint all Evangelicals as political troublemakers who attend tea party rallies, vote for gun rights, and believe in Creation while dismissing global warming. The liberal media, with an obvious anti-God agenda, dismiss God in general and Jesus Christ in particular. To them, Christians, regardless of their denominational affiliations, are irrelevant and in decline and ultimately will just fade away.

The church, however, including Roman Catholic, Pentecostal, Evangelical, and others, is growing faster and often exponentially outside of Europe and North America. The media will tell you Islam is the fastest growing faith, but they are wrong. Christianity is the largest religion in the world, with more than 2.2 billion adherents because of the rapid growth in Latin and South America, Africa, and Asia.[8]

Philip Jenkins, professor of history at Baylor University and author of more than twenty-five books on Christianity, is the author of *The Next Christendom*. His book documents the remarkable expansion of Christianity in what he calls "the global South." He predicts that by 2025, 50 percent of the global Christian population will be in Africa and Latin America.[9]

Because of this, and no surprise to people such as Philip Jenkins, in 2013 the Roman Catholic papal conclave elected Cardinal Jorge Mario Bergoglio of Buenos Aires, Argentina, as pope. Cardinal Bergoglio chose for himself the name Pope Francis, leader of the Roman Catholic Church, the successor of St. Peter.

Christianity is not only surviving in the global South; it is also enjoying a radical revival here, if you look closely enough. For many it is a return to its scriptural roots, an emphasis on the essential truths rather than denominational traditions. It very well could be that even here in America, we are living in truly revolutionary times.

CHAPTER FOUR

Mother Superior

The Pledge of Allegiance

Photo of oil painting *Betsy Ross 1777* by Jean Leon
Gerome Ferris (1863–1930), located presently in a private
collection. Photographic reproduction and original work in
the public domain.

At the beginning of every day at St. Joseph's school, all of us stood, our right hands over our hearts, and recited the Pledge of Allegiance: "I pledge allegiance to the flag of the United States of America and to the republic for which it stands, one nation under God, indivisible, with liberty and justice for all."

Most people don't know that a Baptist preacher, Frank Bellamy, wrote the Pledge of Allegiance. President Benjamin Harrison introduced it to the American public in 1892 in an effort to encourage patriotism. The pledge was purposely to be short, taking only fifteen seconds to recite, and within a few years there were American flags in every schoolroom in the United States, and every school-aged child would recite the pledge daily.

The words *United States of America* were added by Congress in 1923 and *under God* by the urging of President Eisenhower in 1954. At St. Joseph's school, we were certainly both a school as well as a nation under God. While many things have changed since the time I was there, Catholic schools continue to be a strong advocate for education, morality, religious teaching, and conservative, family-oriented values.

School was less complicated then than it seems to be now. There were no computers and no flat-screen monitors, and instead of whiteboards we had green chalkboards. The style of teaching and the expectations were very traditional. The biggest change was when new math was introduced, and for a while we had to contemplate if a number was rational (this completely confused my parents at the time).

The teachers were primarily nuns, and while their average age seemed ancient at the time, they were likely younger than they looked. The younger nuns seemed friendlier than the older ones, but we reasoned it was because they had not had some of us in class yet. There were not enough nuns for all of the classes, so we had a few lay teachers, including one male teacher, Mr. Kloth, whom I eventually had in eighth grade.

There was one teacher per class, and the only nun who did not teach a class was Mother Superior, our term for the principal. I know she must have had a name, but she was Mother Superior before I got there, and

I never heard her called anything else. She retired by the time I was in fifth grade. Interestingly we were able to get through eight years of grade school without a school counselor, a nurse, a dean, an administrative assistant, or a cook. There was no cafeteria, and we all brought our lunches in brown paper bags or, if we were cool, tin lunchboxes with pictures of the Jetsons on the outside.

All the students wore uniforms. There were the typical school bake sales, parents' meetings, and occasional assemblies; however, there was no room large enough for all of us except the church sanctuary. Regardless of the grade, one teacher taught all of the basic subjects. We all took recess and lunch at the same time, and discipline was strict. Other than recess the only official sports program was a basketball team for sixth-, seventh-, and eighth-grade boys.

I was better at baseball and swimming than basketball but tried out for the team when I was in sixth grade anyway because some of my friends were on it. Our coach was Mr. Roberts, who was one of my friends' dad; he also taught a CCD class on Tuesday nights. CCD was an abreviation for Confraternity of Christian Doctrine, which was the official name of the classes established in Rome in 1562. Most of the Catholic boys and girls in town attended the same Catholic school, but there were a few who attended the public schools and therefore had to attend the CCD classes.

I had never heard of the classes before then. When our seventh-grade class at St. Joseph's Catholic School was preparing for Confirmation, Mr. Roberts showed up with three additional boys and a girl, about our age, from his CCD class. They participated in the final preparation class. I was actually surprised there were Catholic students in the public schools. I thought there was some rule about that. I didn't even know that was an option, as certainly neither my brother nor I had a choice. Coach Roberts had been meeting with them on Tuesdays all along.

Sometime in the early spring, a week before the bishop was to be at our church for our Confirmation, we all assembled in the church to get our final instructions. At the time I really was looking forward to Confirmation. It was a rite of passage to me and a sign of maturity. I had become an altar boy back in the fourth grade, and by the seventh grade I was one of the boys who got to assist the priests at both weddings and funerals. Confirmation seemed like the logical next step. For the entire school year, our preparation for Confirmation had become an intentional part of weekly catechism class for the entire seventh grade, all of us utilizing the same Baltimore Catechism I mentioned in the first chapter. I had kept mine in my school desk since the first grade.

Sister Mary Luke peppered our catechism classes with real stories of persecution of Catholics in communist countries. Cuba and the Soviet Union were behind the Iron Curtain, and China was behind a Bamboo Curtain that, while made out of wood, obviously was just as bad.

The Cuban Missile Crisis with President Kennedy and Soviet leader Nikita Khrushchev in October 1962 had taken place only a few years prior, so stories about Catholic persecution in Cuba made great commentary. Sister Mary Luke made it sound like only Catholics faced persecution. I found out later that while it was Catholics in Cuba, it was Orthodox Christians in the Soviet Union; millions of Evangelicals, Pentecostals, and other Protestants had been persecuted in China and North Korea. Regardless of the lack of transparency in Sister Mary Luke's commentary, we could all see that suffering for the faith indeed was a reality.

What piqued my interest even then was how Confirmation was connected to Pentecost, as recorded in the Bible in the book of Acts:

> They saw what seemed to be tongues of fire that separated and came to rest on each of them. All of them were filled with the Holy Spirit and began to speak in other tongues as the Spirit enabled them. (Acts 2:2-3)

We never learned much about the Holy Spirit. For some reason the Second Vatican Council changed His name from the Holy Ghost to the Holy Spirit but didn't communicate a reason to us students in the classroom. It would be another fifteen years before I heard about the Holy Spirit from my charismatic friends.

The Baltimore Catechism taught that there were seven sacraments. By the time I was in seventh grade, I had received three: baptism, penance, and the Holy Eucharist. Confirmation was next, and the Baltimore Catechism said the sacrament would strengthen our faith:

> **Q. 604. Give an example of how the Sacramental grace aids us, for instance, in Confirmation and Penance?**
>
> **A. The end of Confirmation is to strengthen us in our faith. When we are tempted to deny our religion by word or deed, the Sacramental Grace of Confirmation is given to us and helps us to cling to our faith and firmly profess it.**

Church history tells us that long before there was the Roman Catholic sacrament of Confirmation, the church celebrated Pentecost. Even before the church was established, Pentecost was a well-known and very celebrated Jewish feast, particularly during the time of Jesus and the apostles.

Pentecost is actually the Greek name for the Feast of Weeks, called Shavuot in Hebrew, which celebrated the giving of the Law to Israel. The Greek word for Pentecost (*Pentēkostē*) literally means "the fiftieth" day.

Pentecost, the event described in the second chapter of Acts, was the beginning of the church. After Jesus's resurrection but before His ascension, He told His disciples to wait in Jerusalem:

> But you will receive power when the Holy Spirit comes
> on you; and you will be my witnesses in Jerusalem, and
> in all Judea and Samaria, and to the ends of the earth.
> (Acts 1:8)

God's timing is perfect, and we shouldn't be surprised. When the Holy Spirit descended on Pentecost, there were "devout Jews from every nation" in Jerusalem at the time. These Jews were pilgrims, a word that

19

describes religious visitors. They had been planning on returning home soon after the festival was over.

In very dramatic fashion, the Holy Spirit descended on the 120 faithful. Like a mighty wind (the word *wind* in Hebrew is also the name for *spirit*), the Holy Spirit separated into individual tongues of fire on the 120. Some of these included the remaining eleven apostles; Mary, the mother of Jesus; and His brothers. For the first time in history, the Holy Spirit indwelled the entire group, which had been praying and waiting as Jesus had instructed them. They all began to speak in other languages, and the crowds in the street below them were able to hear and understand what they said.

This story of Pentecost, with the apostles and others gathered in the upper room, is well known. It can be confusing for some, with the "visible tongues of fire," the "mighty rushing wind," and the "speaking in other tongues." People often debate these events not in regard to their authenticity but considering their modern equivalence. Nevertheless, Pentecost was the beginning of this movement we call Christianity.

At this gathering Peter stood up and addressed the crowd. His sermon was full of passion, logic, reason, and wisdom. This fisherman, uneducated and sometimes impetuous, was transformed into a mighty preacher. In just more than six hundred words, and taking no more than about twenty minutes, he converted three thousand Jews from Parthia, Media (Iran), and Elam (Iraq); people from Mesopotamia, Judea, Cappadocia, Pontus and Phrygia (Turkey), Pamphylia, (Greece), Egypt, and the areas of Libya around Cyrene; and visitors from Rome. These were the very first converts to Christianity. These men and women were the original Christians. The church was born!

The fact that these three thousand were from various nations was no coincidence. It not only confirmed the miracle of tongues, wherein the Holy Spirit gave the gift of various languages to the church, but also enabled these three thousand to take Christianity back to their homelands.

CHAPTER FIVE

Jews and Gentiles

There is neither Jew nor Gentile, neither slave nor free, nor is there male and female, for you are all one in Christ Jesus.
—Galatians 3:28

Photo of Ariel Sharon at the Battle of Abu-Ageila in 1967.
Photographic reproduction and original work in the
public domain.

Roaming Catholics

It was the end of the school year. Nineteen sixty-seven was also the end of an era, as I was getting ready to graduate from eighth grade at St. Joseph's Catholic School. Looking back, I had a great education, but at the time it seemed like the nuns had spent too much time on handwriting and spelling. We boys never seemed to be as good as the girls in spelling. In addition we had years of classes in geography, history, and mathematics, and, of course, our weekly catechism.

The year 1967 was also the time of an armed conflict we refer to now as the Six-Day War between the Arabs and the Israelis. Because it was such a short war, and I was pretty young, I don't remember too much about the events. The only name I remember was Moshe Dayan, who was easy to pick out on television with the patch over his left eye.

I recently read a biography of this amazing man, whose life bridged the gap between the old Ottoman Empire and the modern state of Israel. I learned he and some of the other founders of the State of Israel, such as Golda Meir, were not religious Jews. They didn't even believe in God; they were atheists. When I think of Israel, it's impossible for me to think of it apart from the amazing stories of Moses and the Ten Commandments or the parting of the Red Sea. These people were in the pages of this incredible story of God's covenant, including a people that believed in the God of Abraham, Isaac, and Jacob. It's too bad people like Moshe Dayan couldn't have seen the hand of God in the rebirth of Israel or their success in the Six-Day War.

We know from the Bible as well as history that the early church was Jewish. While there were Gentile converts included in the three thousand on the day of Pentecost, they were all Jewish in faith. This would mean all of the men had been circumcised and followed the Law; the wives followed their husbands, taught the customs to their children, and were responsible for all the preparation as well as lighting the candles on the festival days. The women would keep kosher kitchens, preparing food for their families in the manner the rabbis had declared.

These early Christians were familiar and often well versed in the Torah. They were aware of the scripture that pointed to a coming Messiah but had limited knowledge of the life and teachings of Jesus.

Soon there would be a learned and zealous man named Saul, a soon-to-be-convert to Christianity, whose rich and inspired letters would explain better the new religion. This Saul, whom we now know as Paul, would write fourteen of the twenty-seven books of the New Testament.

In the absence of any particular new teaching on how they were to structure their gatherings, these early Christians would have relied on their Jewish traditions. The psalms, originally all songs written for Israel, would often be a portion of their worship. There were two official officers in the new church: elders and deacons. The elders would be the teachers and would be responsible for teaching and celebrating all they knew about Jesus and His teachings. The liturgy the Catholic Church would recognize in a few hundred years was not yet developed. There were no priests, no church hierarchy, and no established order of worship.

Soon Paul and others of the remaining eleven apostles would begin to plant churches throughout the Mediterranean. The Gentile population of the church started to grow rapidly. For centuries Gentiles had been attracted to this religion of the Jews and their one God. However, for men conversion required circumcision, a painful procedure most avoided. With Christianity a Gentile could embrace fully this God of the Jews and believe in the death, burial, and resurrection of Jesus without needing to be circumcised or become a Jew first.

By the fifth century, we had the first evidence of a contemporary liturgical prayer, *"Santus, Santus, Santus"* (Latin for "holy, holy, holy"), being used as part of the worship service. Local tradition says that in AD 440, a violent earthquake shook Constantinople during a service, lifting a child into the air. According to this folklore, the people cried out in Greek, *"Kyrie eleison,"* or "Lord have mercy!" and the child gently floated back to the ground. Within a dozen years, this exclamation in Greek was incorporated into the liturgy (the official ceremony) and put to music.[10]

It's natural for people to find comfort and a sense of security in knowing the pattern of greeting, prayer, song, reading, and sermon when they gather together at their place of worship. However, patterns, familiarity, and tradition often become religious standards that become hard-and-fast requirements. For example, a few years ago, I had the opportunity to officiate at the Sunday service and was to bring the morning message in a nondenominational church. The worship director and I had a brief meeting during the week to go over the various elements of the service, and because of a few special features that weekend it looked like we were going to be pressed for time unless I shortened my sermon.

Like most other preachers, I thought there must be a better way to free up a few minutes than cut back on the homily, so the worship director and I decided to eliminate the Lord's Prayer. That next Sunday the service started on time. The music and the special vocalists were superb, and it looked like it was going to be a great morning until we got to the part where the congregation normally and (obviously to me later) for years had said the Lord's Prayer aloud.

A murmur started immediately when we skipped it, and I could tell when I gave my sermon that a few attendees were quite upset about something. Right after the service, when I was greeting some of the parishioners, one woman came up to me and said, "Pastor, you may not realize that you committed this error, but you omitted the Lord's Prayer."

I told her I knew, but before I could explain my reasoning she cut me off and said, "We have to say the Lord's Prayer every Sunday, as even Jesus said, 'When you pray, pray in this manner.'"

Some traditions start coincidentally and even unintentionally, but they become the very religious fabric people relate to each week and are very difficult to change without creating an affront to those who have grown accustomed to them.

CHAPTER SIX

All Roads Lead to Rome

Has anybody here seen my old friend Abraham—
Can you tell me where he's gone?
He freed a lot of people, but it seems the
good die young
But I just looked around and he's gone.
—"Abraham, Martin, and John," by Dick Holler, 1968

Sacco di Roma of 455 AD by Karl Briullov, circa 1835. Oil
on canvas, presently on display at the Tretyakov Gallery,
Moscow. Photographic reproduction and original work in
the public domain.

I am a member of the generation that saw three major American leaders—great patriots all—fall within a five-year period, from 1963 to 1968. We were in the middle of a spelling bee in our fifth-grade class at St. Joseph's Catholic School when we heard the announcement that someone had shot President Kennedy in Dallas. The news was upsetting, and I remember seeing the face of our teacher, Sister Mary Dominick, and how personally she was taking it.

I don't think all fifth graders in the United States were quite as informed as we Catholic schoolchildren were on the historical election of this American-Catholic president. My parents were and had been Republicans but enthusiastically embraced Jack Kennedy; his beautiful wife, Jacqueline, and the rest of the Kennedys. As a family we knew the story of PT-109 and were familiar with the entire Kennedy clan, including Caroline's pony named Macaroni.

Since everyone in my family and nearly everyone I knew was Catholic, I didn't fully understand what the big deal was to have a Catholic president. However, because the evening news continually had stories that questioned Kennedy's ability or desire to govern independently of the pope, his presidency had a role in educating me as to the role of the pope in Rome and the interesting mix of religion and politics.

Growing up Catholic I was constantly being taught about Rome. Our history books, the nuns, and all of their stories portrayed Rome as this historic, majestic, and holy capital of the world. I also learned about St. Peter, to whom Jesus had given the keys to the kingdom of heaven and who also was said to have been the first pope.

Much later I learned about the sack of Rome in AD 410 by Alarac I, king of the Visigoths. Rome's decline had started a century before Alarac, and it continued until it was no longer a fitting place for the heads of the church or the heads of state. Once-powerful Rome was no longer able to protect itself, let alone lead and protect the rest of the empire.

Earlier, from AD 324 to 330, Emperor Constantine had built a new capital for the empire more than 850 miles east, strategically located between the Black and the Aegean Seas. This site of the ancient Greek city Byzantium would survive the fall of Rome and the Western portion of the empire and be the capital of what we sometimes call the Eastern Roman Empire or the Byzantine Empire for more than one thousand years. Massive gates and impregnable walls fortified this new Rome. It became the center of not only the empire but also Christian theology and learning. Unlike what I learned in our history and catechism classes at St. Joseph Catholic School, it was the East and not the West that led both the empire and the church. It was Constantinople and not Rome that, for much of this period of Christian formation, led the church in both the formation of doctrine and teaching.

Some of the notable theologians and teachers from the East included:

- St. Anthony the Great of Egypt (AD 251–356).
- St. Basil the Great of Caesarea (AD 330–379).
- St. Nicholas (AD 270–343), the original Santa Claus, who was from an area on the southern coast of Turkey.
- St. Athanasius (AD 298–373), bishop of Alexandria and a profound theologian.
- St. Gregory of Cappadocia (AD 329–390), known as Gregory the Theologian—the leader of the Second Ecumenical Council called by Emperor Flavius Theodosius.
- St. John Chrysostom (AD 347–407), the patriarch of Constantinople and author of the Divine Liturgy.

Rome, the Eternal City, was desperate for protection and stability and remained so until Charlemagne, also called Charles the Great, became the first ruler of the Holy Roman Empire. Charlemagne united much of the former western portion of the Roman Empire. Almost four hundred years after the fall of Rome, on December 25, AD 800, Charlemagne knelt in prayer at the old St. Peter's Basilica in Rome. Pope Leo III made him emperor by placing a gold crown on his head and naming him the head of the Holy Roman Empire.

In Constantinople relationships between the Latin West and the Greek (Byzantine) Eastern churches had been strained for years, but crowning Charlemagne as emperor was a serious insult to the Byzantine Church and the patriarch of Constantinople, who didn't recognize the right of Leo III to crown a head of state. In addition Empress Irene of Constantinople was clearly upset that Charlemagne had been crowned emperor of Rome,[11] as she believed she was the actual and only emperor of the remaining former Roman Empire.

The conflict between the Eastern and Western portions of the Roman Empire, the fall of Rome, or the failure of any of its popes was not a story students heard in Catholic schools. For Catholics Rome was and would always be the Holy City, the location of the Vatican, and the seat of power of the Catholic Church. It was also the place where, Catholics are taught, St. Peter was the first pope and was crucified upside down, and where his successors were the true rulers of the church and the arbiters of all religious dogma and knowledge.

Looking through the history books, however, told me a different story. For example, it is very clear that for the first one thousand years, five important bishops, called patriarchs, jointly ruled the church. These five senior bishops formed a *pentarchy* (*pente* is a Greek word for five) based on the establishment of administrative regions within the Roman Empire.

These patriarchs were located in five very significant cities in the Roman Empire, including Jerusalem, where the church was born; Antioch, where believers were first called Christians; Alexandria, one of most important Roman cities in Africa; Constantinople, the capital of the Eastern Roman Empire from the fourth to the fifteenth century; and Rome, the original capital of the empire and the city that experienced a rebirth during the late Middle Ages and into the Italian Renaissance.

These patriarchs originally considered themselves equals, the rulers of their respective geographical areas, and rarely interfered in matters of faith outside of their jurisdictions. In addition, when major decisions regarding matters of faith were necessary, the church would come together in councils with a large gathering of bishops, including some but not all of these patriarchs.

History tells us the patriarch of Rome, by the end of the fourth century, was calling himself pope (Pope Siricius, AD 334–399). The bishop of Rome was also one of the five patriarchs and always garnered great respect and honor whenever the church came together in one of the ecumenical councils. However, the patriarch of Rome often did not lead nor even attend some of the churchwide councils. This was true even after Pope Leo the Great (400–461) bravely met Attila the Hun and proclaimed the primacy of the bishop of Rome based on his succession from the apostle Peter.

The Pope, then called the patriarch of Rome, was not one of the 318 bishops and theologians who attended the First Council of Nicaea in AD 325. Emperor Constantine actually called this council, and the bishop of Cordova, a man named Ossius (Hosius), presided over not only the council but also the Councils of Antioch (also in AD 325) and Serdica (in AD 343).[12]

The second ecumenical council was in Constantinople in AD 381, with 150 bishops in attendance. However, the patriarch of Rome, Damasus I, did not attend or send any delegates from the West.

The lack of attendance by these early bishops or patriarchs of Rome, however, in no way diminished the very important role many of these men of God played in the development of orthodox doctrine and their careful watch over heresy not only in the early church (i.e., second through fourth centuries) but also through the Middle Ages.

Today nearly one billion people consider themselves Roman Catholic, and nearly all of them acknowledge the role of the pope as the head of the church. They hold to the traditional teaching that the modern-day popes are all successors of the apostle Peter, who founded the church in Rome and set up the line of succession that continues to this day.

While we have had good popes and bad popes, we'll look, in some of the following chapters, a little more into the role the apostle Peter actually had in the early church and how the popular teaching of the Roman Catholic Church developed.

CHAPTER SEVEN

Pax Romana

The Eternal City and Headquarters for the Church

St. Constantine and St. Helena around the Holy Cross.
Oil on canvas by Vasey, 1870, Russia. Photographic
reproduction and original work in the public domain.

My brother was two years younger than I was and was hoping against hope that Sister Mary Luke would retire from teaching sixth grade at St. Joseph's Catholic School before he was in her class. There are a lot of stories I could tell about the nuns (and I'm about to tell one), but I have to admit they were actually pretty good teachers. They were all, of course, strict disciplinarians, and each of them could throw a chalkboard eraser twenty-five to thirty feet, as if they were football great Johnny Unitas throwing a pass to John Mackey. The difference was that John Mackey, a tight end for the Baltimore Colts, typically knew when the flying object was coming at him. At St. Joseph's school, we students never knew when the eraser might be coming. Typically the boys would be the targets, and the erasers would ricochet off of our blue uniform shirts, leaving large blotches of white chalk dust as reminders of the egregious sins we had committed.

Sister Mary Luke had a good right arm and could throw a chalk-filled eraser with the best of them. Her claim to fame, however, that made my brother and others hope for an early retirement offer from the bishop was her complete lack of tolerance of noise. There was no Christian charity in the old woman when it came to noise. Any noise in the class would send her over the edge, whether it was a student ripping a page out of a spiral notebook or accidentally dropping a pencil on the floor. She would immediately stop the class and begin to moan, shake her head, and find the source of her irritation.

I remember Sister Mary Luke also for her midsemester projects that allowed us to spend some time in class building things out of wood and Styrofoam. I jumped at the chance of using some of the plastic medieval knights, complete with a crusader castle, that I had received a few years before at Christmas. To change it up a little, instead of a castle I put the knights in a Roman fort and built some ramparts and watchtowers. My medieval knights now looked more like Roman soldiers, with tunics and spears; it was a vast improvement over the out-of-the-box appearance of the crusaders of the eleventh and twelfth centuries.

I can't remember if I received an E, a VG, or a G (for some reason the Catholic schools didn't use the A through F grading system) on the

Roman fort project, but Sister Mary Luke used it as an opportunity to talk about the *pax Romana*, or Roman peace. This was an honor to me, of course, but I had expected it, as anything Rome related was a common teaching theme at St. Joseph's Catholic School. To the nuns Rome was and would forever be the Eternal City. Their teaching about it and fondness for it were consistent and unwavering.

Later, as an adult and a developing history buff, I wanted to find out how the small Christian sect that started in Jerusalem but spread out through the empire went from being a persecuted minority to the official religion of Rome. The nuns always taught that the history of Rome had been glorious. From their perspective, the church had made it famous, and the pope had always ruled over the entire church from Rome. They told stories of how even kings and emperors had to get permission from the pope before they could be crowned.

History tells us the transformation from a persecuted church to the official religion of Rome took only about seventy years, starting around the beginning of the fourth century AD.

If you visit Rome today, you can see the Triumphal Arch of Constantine, which has a plaque dedicating it to Constantine's victory over a rival Caesar named Maxentius. Constantine had become the emperor of Rome in AD 306. According to legend Emperor Constantine, whose mother, Helena, was a Christian, looked up to the sky just prior to his battle with Maxentius and saw a cross, along with the words "in this sign conquer" in Greek. Constantine had his troops put the first two letters of the name "Christ", Chi-Rho, on the shields. At that time, Chi-Rho was already a known symbol of Christianity. Constantine went on to win the decisive battle against Maxentius at the Milvian Bridge in AD 312, and after this battle was the sole ruler of the entire empire.

As a result of this event, Constantine embraced or, at a minimum, favored Christianity. He officially ended persecution, and in AD 380, fewer than seventy years after the battle at the Milvian Bridge, the Roman emperor Theodosius made Christianity the state religion. In his proclamation he officially called the new religion Catholic—a term that in both Greek and Latin meant "universal."

Constantine was not a model Christian. He continued to retain his title, Pontifex Maximus, as head of the pagan state religion, and he had his enemies murdered. After Theodosius made Christianity the official religion of Rome, the bishop of Rome (soon to be called pope) and the church had great power. And it is true what they say: power corrupts, and absolute power corrupts absolutely.

While there may have been many instances of corruption in the early church because of its power and close alignment with the state, there were also instances of humility and sacrifice and passionate calls for repentance and holiness. One example occurred immediately after Emperor Theodosius had made Christianity the official religion. The archbishop of Milan was Aurelius Ambrosius, better known as St. Ambrose. He was a good friend of Emperor Theodosius, but when he heard that Theodosius had slaughtered more than seven thousand people in Thessalonica in AD 390, he excommunicated the emperor and told him he needed to repent. According to many historical documents, Ambrose told Theodosius to "imitate David in his repentance as he had imitated him in his guilt."[13] Theodosius complied.

Here in the United States, we have had religious freedom and, in most of the Western world, a legacy of religious pluralism for more than two centuries. However, people today can still feel intimidated by friends and family when they choose to follow Christ in a manner that is different from others. This is most unfortunate. Just as we had the early witnesses, called martyrs or saints, who were willing to die for their faith, there were Americans who were willing to die for the rights we have today, including the freedom of religion.

For some of us who may be a little more prepared, when others question our religious beliefs we have opportunities to share not only our beliefs but the reasons for them and a bit of history. Understanding the history of the church provides answers that can help a person grow in faith, in understanding, and in Christ.

Oh...my brother, Dave, did end up spending his sixth-grade year in Sister Mary Luke's class. Having me as his older brother wasn't necessarily a good thing. However, he actually learned a thing or two from the elderly nun and found the experience wasn't as bad as he had thought it would be. We heard she retired a few years after that, and she was probably just as glad that she didn't have either one of us in her class anymore.

CHAPTER EIGHT

The Gettysburg Address

The Nicene Creed of AD 325

Icon of Emperor Constantine and the bishops at the First
Council of Nicaea (AD 325), holding the Nicene Creed.
Photographic reproduction and original work in the public
domain.

One of the fifth-grade teachers at St. Joseph's Catholic School was Mrs. Van Dam. The school had two fifth-grade classes with about thirty students in each, but I was not in her class. She was young and married, and both of these characteristics separated her from most of the other teachers, who were all Dominican nuns.

However, Mrs. Van Dam would often come in and teach one of our subjects so our teacher, Sister Mary Dominick, could teach the other fifth-grade class religion, using the indispensible Baltimore Catechism.

Mrs. Van Dam typically taught us math, but she also liked history and got permission from Sister Mary Dominick and our Principal to put on a play portraying the life of President Abraham Lincoln. Part of the assignment would be that we would all learn by heart the Gettysburg Address.

My part in *The Rail Splitter* (the name we gave to the play) was very minor. Actually I had two parts, as I played the man who ran out of the theater to say, "Someone shot President Lincoln at the Ford Theater." I also played a bailiff, or the court assistant, in the first scene, when we first saw young Abraham Lincoln as a lawyer in an Illinois courtroom. The judge had a speaking part; I just had to stand there.

Since I obviously wasn't the talent on the stage, I decided I would do a good job at memorizing the Gettysburg Address. It was a challenge for a fifth grader, but as it contained only 272 words, and supposedly we could recite it in fewer than two minutes, I rose to the occasion. This wasn't the first time I'd had to commit something to memory. Catholics were big on formal prayers, and because we had to remember them or because we just said them so often, I soon committed them to memory. By the second grade, every Catholic schoolboy and schoolgirl could recite the Our Father, which non-Catholics refer to as the Lord's Prayer; the Hail Mary; and the Act of Confession.

The Gettysburg Address continues to be memorable, though I haven't tried to recite it recently. I do remember at the time seeing the words "the world will little note, nor long remember what we say here, but it can never forget what they did here" and thinking how much the world did remember what Abraham Lincoln had said that day in Gettysburg.

The other things we would recite often but didn't fully memorize were the creeds. There were two that we used often: the Nicene Creed and the Apostles' Creed.

The Nicene Creed has an extraordinary history. It goes back to the time of Constantine, whom I mentioned in the previous chapter. Constantine was the emperor of Rome and a convert to Christianity. He wanted his empire unified and was alarmed by a number of disputes, schisms, and even heresies that existed in the church at the time.

Constantine called the Council of Nicaea in AD 325 and assembled a group of bishops at what we now know was the First Ecumenical Council of the Church. Scholars estimate that from 220 to as many as 318 bishops attended. Constantine had invited many more, but we can excuse their absences, as travel back in the fourth century was difficult. In addition the persecution of the Christians had been very severe in parts of the empire and had only recently ended, so traveling was not a likely part of the bishops' job description.

The eastern region of the empire was fully represented; three of the high-ranking patriarchs of Alexandria, Antioch, and Jerusalem were in attendance.[14] The patriarch, or bishop, of Rome, Pope Sylvester, who ruled from AD 314 to AD 335, did not attend the Council of Nicaea; however, he did send some representatives.

At the time of the council, there were a number of competing doctrines in the church. These ranged from articles of the faith concerning the true divinity of Christ and the nature and validity of baptisms to the roles of the bishops and priests and the celebration of Easter.

Both Constantine and the bishops had a number of key objectives. The first was an end to schisms. The second was a decision on the controversial teachings of a priest named Arius. The third was ultimately to achieve peace and unity within both the church and the empire.

While the bishops could have created a definitive document that clearly defined and embraced all of the various teachings, canons, sacraments, and doctrines of the church, they surprised most people at the time, and historians today, by carefully crafting a short creed that summarized what it meant to be a Christian.

The entire council declared and ratified these simple beliefs of the Christian faith in the Nicene Creed. Since that time, nearly 1,700 years later, the creed has been the simple litmus test for what we consider orthodox—not Orthodox as in the branch of Eastern Christianity, but orthodox from the Greek root *orthos*, meaning "right, true, or straight."

Here, in its entirety, is the Nicene Creed:

> We believe in one God,
> the Father, the Almighty,
> maker of heaven and earth,
> of all that is, seen and unseen.
> We believe in one Lord, Jesus Christ,
> the only son of God,
> eternally begotten of the Father,
> God from God, Light from Light,
> true God from true God,
> begotten, not made,
> of one being with the Father.
> Through him all things were made.
> For us and for our salvation
> he came down from heaven:
> by the power of the Holy Spirit
> he became incarnate from the Virgin Mary,
> and was made man.
> For our sake he was crucified under Pontius Pilate,
> he suffered death and was buried,
> and rose again on the third day
> in accordance with the Scriptures.
> He ascended into heaven
> and is seated at the right hand of the Father.
> He will come again in glory
> to judge the living and the dead
> and his kingdom will have no end.

We believe in the Holy Spirit, the Lord, the giver of life,
who proceeds from the Father [and the Son].
With the Father and the Son
he is worshipped and glorified.
He has spoken through the Prophets.
We believe in one holy catholic and apostolic church.
We acknowledge one baptism for the forgiveness of sins.
We look for the resurrection of the dead,
and the life of the world to come. Amen.

This simple creed is what we believe! Catholic, Orthodox, Presbyterian, Methodist, Pentecostal, Baptist, Lutheran—all Christian churches embrace the same creed. There are only thirty-five lines in the creed, just 226 words. Approximately 60 percent of it is about the nature of Jesus. In the creed we state our belief in His oneness with the Father, His virgin birth, His death for our sins, His resurrection, and His second coming.

There is no mention in the Nicene Creed of the bishops, the pastors, or the priests. There is not one word on the governing authority of the church, whether it is a pope, a bishop, or a deacon board. There are no words regarding the Mass, worship specifics, or special liturgies. There is only one line that refers to the church at all: "We believe in one holy catholic and apostolic church."

This is what Jesus prayed for as well:

I do not ask for these only, but also for those who will believe in me through their word, that they may all be one, just as you, Father, are in me, and I in you, that they also may be in us, so that the world may believe that you have sent me. The glory that you have given me I have given to them, that they may be one even as we are one, I in them and you in me, that they may become perfectly one, so that the world may know that you sent me and loved them even as you loved me. (John 17:20–23, ESV)

The word *holy* refers to the fact that the church is to be separated or holy unto God and is in fact the Body of Christ. The word *catholic* is from the Greek word *katholikos,* meaning "universal." The word *apostolic* refers to the fact that the teachings of the apostles are the foundation of the church. Finally the word church, is from the Greek word *ekklesia,* which is a compound word meaning "to call" and "out from and to." In other words, the church, or *ekklesia,* is those whom God calls out from the world and calls to Him.

CHAPTER NINE

Baptism

In the Name of the Father, and of the Son, and of the Holy Ghost

—Matthew 28:19

"Wade in the Water." Postcard of a river baptism in New
Bern, North Carolina, around the turn of the twentieth
century. Photographic image in the public domain.

I was baptized when I was ten days old at St. John Bosco church. St. John Bosco is an inner-city, primarily Polish Roman Catholic Church named for a nineteenth-century saint from Turin, Italy, who dedicated his life to helping youth. As I was only ten days old, I don't remember my baptism.

I was also baptized in a swimming pool along with my wife and a small group of about eight people at a church camp in South Carolina when I was in my twenties. I remember the day very well. I remember the excitement, the feeling of going under the water, the sweet surrender of my soul to God's will for my life, and the minister's simple prayers.

Today, as a pastor, I often get the opportunity to baptize people, including something we get to do in South Florida: baptism in the Atlantic Ocean. When the waves are fierce, we stay close to the shore and let the surf do most of the work.

The history of baptism in the church is interesting and typically one of the most controversial teachings. Today there is a great deal of emphasis in many denominations on baptism, and over the centuries people have been baptized in many different ways.

The Bible actually has a lot to say about baptism. We see in Matthew, chapter three, the coming of John the Baptist, a first cousin of Jesus, calling people to repentance and baptizing them in the River Jordan.

The word *baptize* is from the Greek word *baptizo* and means "to dip or immerse under water." However, the word also can mean "to clean with water." The Greek word was used, for example, in the way cloth was dyed: it would be immersed under water with pigment. Another example would be how a blacksmith would *baptizo* a piece of hot iron in water to cool it quickly and therefore make it stronger.

The Jewish followers of John the Baptist, who were called to repent of their sins, already knew a lot about baptism. In the Jewish culture, ritual washings, or baptisms, were also one of the final steps for Gentile converts to Judaism. They would be baptized (called a *mikvah*) "into Moses" by symbolically recalling the crossing by the Israelites of the Red Sea.

In the early church people who were converted "into Christ" were baptized typically by being immersed in water. We know this because we have historical evidence from the time of the apostles, including excavations of baptismals that are deep enough for an adult to be immersed fully. We also know from first-century writings that the bishops could grant permission for water to be poured only if there wasn't sufficient or deep water available.

During the first few centuries, new Christian believers would receive special instruction for an entire year. These new believers were called Catechumens, and after their instruction the church would have a huge celebration, typically right around Palm Sunday, when these new believers were baptized, given white robes, and became full members of the church.

At that time baptism was a rite of initiation with great symbolic meaning, but it was not directly tied to the forgiveness of sins. Many Catechumens, for example, who were not yet baptized went to the Roman Colosseum and faced martyrdom confident of their salvation.

However, by the fourth century, Christians generally associated baptism with the forgiveness of all sins. As a result many people would delay their baptisms to gain maximum effect and wash away many years of sin. Emperor Constantine the Great, for example, delayed his baptism until his deathbed. The leaders of the church saw a great moral danger in delaying baptism, and fortunately for them another teaching—that baptism was necessary for salvation—became popular. St. Augustine (AD 354–430) had written, "How many rascals are saved by being baptized on their deathbeds? And how many sincere Catechumens die unbaptized, and are thus lost forever!"[15]

As a result of these dilemmas and Augustine's teaching, two new Catholic doctrines—the doctrine of necessity (that baptism is necessary) and the doctrine of forgiveness (that baptism forgives original sin)—officially emerged. Since the mortality rate for infants was very high, soon babies were being baptized within a few days of birth. By the end of the fourth century, baptism, as an initial step of initiation into the church, split into two sacraments: baptism for infants and then a later confirmation for adolescents and adults, replacing what was typically an adult baptism via immersion that accomplished both rites. In the Eastern or

Orthodox Church, babies are still baptized by immersion rather than being sprinkled, or by having water poured over their foreheads.

By the sixteenth century, many of the reformers began to look at infant baptism in light of both early church history as well as the teachings in the Bible and encouraged each other to be baptized again. These Anabaptists, as they were called, restarted the practice in the church of what we know today as believers' baptism, which is practiced in many of our Evangelical churches.

Not all Christians baptize the same way, nor do all Christian denominations recognize each other's baptisms. However, many Evangelical Christians believe that water baptism identifies the believer with the Godhead—Father, Son, and Holy Spirit—as we are commanded in Matthew 28:19 to "Therefore go and make disciples of all nations, baptizing them in the name of the Father and of the Son and of the Holy Spirit."

Further, water baptism identifies the believer with Christ in His death, burial, and resurrection.

> Or don't you know that all of us who were baptized into Christ Jesus were baptized into his death? We were therefore buried with him through baptism into death in order that, just as Christ was raised from the dead through the glory of the Father, we too may live a new life. (Rom. 6:3–4).

While some may believe baptism is only symbolic, we also need to remember it was one of the two commonly recognized sacraments of the church. Historically sacraments were viewed as "an outward and visible sign of an inward and spiritual grace given to us, ordained by Christ himself."[16] Baptism is the manner by which the church fulfills the commandment of Jesus to "make disciples...and baptize them" as well as for the believer to identify himself or herself with his or her new life in Christ.

CHAPTER TEN

What is a Catholic?

The Rest We Judge Demented and Insane

—Emperor Theodosius I

St. Anne Parish on Mackinac Island. Original mission dates back to 1670 and Jesuit Father Jacques Marquette. Photo by John Caulton, all rights reserved.

Connie, a friend of mine whose real name is Constantine, is married to a sweet lady named Frankie. If you think having friends by the name of Connie and Frankie is unusual, you can imagine how confusing it is when Connie is the guy and Frankie is the girl.

Connie often tells the story of his time in the service during the Vietnam era. One day at boot camp, his sergeant got all of the men lined up in front of the barracks and then told them, "Men, today is Sunday, and you all will take the opportunity to go to a church service this morning. I want all of you who are Cat-o-licks to go to the right with Father Patrick, and you Protestants go to the left with Reverend Dempsey."

Connie said he just stood there as the rest of his squad filed to the left or the right. His sergeant came up to him, got in his face, and said, "What's with you, Constantine? You some atheist?"

Connie replied, "No, Sergeant, I'm Eastern Orthodox."

The sergeant replied, "Constantine, you're a Protestant."

About a quarter of the people who consider themselves to be of the Christian faith in the United States are Catholics, according to most surveys. Typically these are in reality Roman Catholics, the largest denomination within Christianity.

For most Catholics, to be Catholic means a number of things, including the fact that they were baptized as Catholics, they attend Mass when they go to church, and they acknowledge the pope as the head of the church and priests' abilities to consecrate bread and wine into the body and blood of Jesus Christ.

That above summation is mine based on my observations from my original core Catholic upbringing and from my years of serving as a pastor and talking with people who either presently consider themselves Catholic or recently were active in the Catholic faith.

As we discussed in the previous chapter, the word *catholic* is from the Greek word *katholikos*, meaning "universal." It was officially applied to the church around the fourth century, and we see it in both the Nicene Creed ("We believe in one holy, catholic, and apostolic church") and the Apostles' Creed, which appeared at the end of the fourth century.

In AD 380 the Roman emperor Theodosius made Christianity the state religion, calling the new religion Catholic, with an imperial command:

> All peoples we rule shall practice that religion which the divine Peter the Apostle transmitted to the Romans. We command those persons who follow this rule shall embrace the name of Catholic Christians. The rest, however, whom we judge demented and insane shall sustain the infamy of heretical dogmas, their meeting places shall not receive the name of church, and they shall be smitten.[17]

There were two enemies Emperor Theodosius and some of the bishops were eager to smite. The first was anyone or any group that still adhered to what is referred to as Arianism. Arius was a scholar/priest who lived in the early fourth century and taught that Jesus was not fully God. The Council of Nicaea and the resulting Nicene Creed carefully and very purposefully stated that Jesus was fully God, as He was begotten, not made.

The second enemy was anyone who questioned the authority or the doctrines of the increasingly hierarchical and very powerful group of bishops and patriarchs, one of whom was the bishop of Rome, the pope.

With Theodosius's decree the Catholic Church became the official religion of the Roman Empire. It was no longer a small, minor sect, an offspring of Judaism that the larger pagan population often misunderstood and that Roman authorities persecuted. All inhabitants of the Roman Empire, including citizens, nobles, landowners, peasants, slaves, and strangers, were to "follow this rule [and] shall embrace the name of Catholic Christians."[18]

Imagine for a moment what that meant to the people of the Roman Empire. The emperor required these former pagans, Jews, and assorted Gentiles to be baptized and become faithful in regular church attendance.

For those who were already Christians before the emperor's decree in AD 380, the change was just as dramatic. Because of the large increase in numbers, Christians could no longer all fit into the relatively small house churches that had been popular and safe during the turbulent times of persecution. Instead, and by decree of the emperor, the Roman government provided the newly empowered Catholic Church the basilicas (imperial buildings) that the Roman authorities had used for administrative work as well as pagan celebrations. Needing even more space, the government and the church leaders developed building projects. The wealthy landowners would donate property or sometimes would find it confiscated. People were told to give, often voluntarily but also through compulsion. Soon, every large village and town was home to new beautiful buildings.

Very soon the church was no longer thought of as regular people but as officially the clergy and governing authority. The ranking leaders of the church were the bishops, also called the patriarchs of five important Roman cities: Antioch, Alexandria, Constantinople, Jerusalem, and Rome. These patriarchs were officially in charge of their particular metropolitan areas and the neighboring geographic areas.

The patriarch of Rome took on high honor and the name pope by the sixth century. While during the first one thousand years, these patriarchs shared their power, the pope's rule became supreme after Rome regained its power and prestige as Charlemagne the Great became the head of the Holy Roman Empire and ruled most of Western Europe.

Charlemagne's rise to power changed history, officially reestablished Rome and the West, and erased much of the historical influence of Constantinople and the East that had been extensive since the decline of the western Roman Empire in AD 476.

The clergy grew in power and in numbers. During this era they began to wear special clerical clothes. Earlier, by the end of the second century, the presbyters who led local churches began to be called priests.

Unfortunately and all too often, the Roman emperor and others in power appointed and dismissed bishops, patriarchs, and abbots rather than the appropriate leaders in the church. From time to time, the church would turn the tables on the Roman government and ask even the emperor to repent and fast, but more and more the division between church and state was a fine line that was often blurred.

The need for a standard liturgy grew in the minds of those who felt they were in charge. The thought was that unity of the church would only come about by conformity. Initially there was great variety in Sunday celebrations, language, and customs. In the seventh century, however, Pope Gregory the Great declared that the Latin Mass in Rome was the standard for the Western Church. Latin versus Greek would ultimately contribute to the Great Schism in the church in AD 1054.

As it became more scripted and standardized, the Catholic Mass emphasized the sacrificial aspect of Jesus, focusing on His death on the cross, and grew in importance while the teaching, preaching, and symbolism of the Passover in the Eucharist faded.

The theology of the period stressed Christ's divinity and a harsh divine judgment on all people who violated both the moral code as well as the laws of the church. This theology led to the people feeling less worthy and less likely to approach God, and instead to look to the church as the go-between between God and man. As a result there was a gradual separation between the clergy and laity. The church taught that the clergy were closer to God, holy, and worthy, while the people were separated from God, unholy, and unworthy of God's love.

However, all through this time, God was still on the throne. The Holy Spirit had been poured out on Pentecost. The jailer had asked the apostle Peter (the first pope, as the Catholic Church later taught), "What must I do to be saved?"

Peter replied, "Believe in the Lord Jesus Christ and you will be saved—you and your household" (Acts 16:30–31).

These early Catholic Christians believed in the Lord Jesus Christ. Over the years their theology, their rites, and some of their other beliefs changed; however, at the heart of the Catholic Church was the belief in the Virgin Birth, the sacrificial death, and the glorious resurrection of the Lord Jesus Christ.

CHAPTER ELEVEN

Early Mass

The Public Duty

Interior of St. Peter's in Rome, oil on canvas painting by
Wilheim van Ehrenberg, AD 1671. Location: Museum of
Fine Arts, Ghent. Photographic reproduction and original
work in the public domain.

Each morning my brother and I would walk about a half block down the street, to the corner, to wait for the school bus. The bus would pick us up at 6:45 a.m. and drop us off in front of the school by 7:00 a.m.

St. Joseph's Catholic School was adjacent to St. Joseph's parish, and since school didn't start until 7:50 a.m., all of us students who arrived early by bus were required to attend the 7:00 a.m. Mass. Over the years that my brother and I attended St. Joseph's, we probably attended more than eight hundred Masses. There was nothing necessarily remarkable about any one of them; I don't remember any particular message, and they all blend together. However, I also don't remember ever getting into any trouble while I was in the church attending Mass, which was likely the primary reason the nuns insisted we be inside rather than outside of the church.

The Mass that Roman Catholics know and love has undergone more changes in the past forty to fifty years than in the previous thousand. However, for the faithful Roman Catholic, the Mass is essential in his or her faith. It is the necessary ingredient in being a Roman Catholic.

It is most likely the rich liturgy, the history, and the traditions of the Mass that draw millions of people into their local Roman Catholic churches. For most, going to Mass is essential, and it is the only way to feel like they have attended church. The Mass is described officially in very symbolic and theological language. For the people in the pews, it is like the comfortable sweater or slippers that are part of their Saturday evening or Sunday morning routine.

Catholics go to Mass, genuflect when they get to the pew of their choice, and fully embrace the tradition and the order of the Mass. They will stand at the beginning; the procession; the opening sign of the cross; and the readings, psalm, and Gospel. They will sit during the brief homily. They will stand and have no need to look at the pamphlet to say aloud the Apostles' Creed, because over the years they have memorized it without any particular effort. They will sit through the offertory, kneel for the consecration and Lord's Prayer, and participate in communion, and then the priest will dismiss them.

If the particular Roman Catholic is old enough to remember the changes brought about by Vatican II, he or she may be able to recall the Mass being celebrated in Latin, with the priest facing the altar set back against the wall. Since Vatican II much has changed. The church now encourages the people to participate more, and the priest recites the liturgy in the language of the people rather than in Latin.

While the Mass is centuries old, it did evolve over time and was not a part of the weekly celebration or the worship services of the early church.

Most people have heard the word *liturgy*, and the Roman Catholic Church has a well-described and very prescribed liturgy that must be followed. Many other churches have rich liturgies and could be described as liturgical, including not only the Greek Orthodox (which continues to observe an ancient tradition) but also the Episcopal and Anglican Churches as well as the Lutheran, Methodist, and Presbyterian Churches.

This word, *liturgy*, is taken originally from the Greek word *leitourgia*. A hint to the origin of the Mass is found in the word itself, as *leitourgia* is a Greek composite word meaning originally a "public duty." For the first three centuries, geographically dispersed churches recited various rites and prescribed unique prayers and particular readings.

These prayers, rites, and ceremonies were anything but uniform until the Roman Empire required a more standard, official, and approved liturgy. The church as well saw a benefit in approving the liturgy, so throughout all of the empire and everywhere that Christians were gathering, they used the same prayers, intercessions, and readings.

While there is nothing wrong with conforming to a particular liturgy, conformity quickly became the way to determine unity. If a local parish priest or a bishop determined or gave permission for the use of a different liturgy, often those who were suspicious of motives questioned the decision. Ultimately, the church leaders approved specific liturgies, and in the Western part of the church all were exclusively in Latin. It wasn't until 1964 that nearly seven hundred million people who called themselves Roman Catholic would be able to hear the liturgy, or what they refer to as the Mass, celebrated in their own language.

CHAPTER TWELVE

Thou Art Peter

"And upon this rock..."

Frescoes of the Brancacci Chapel in Santa Maria del Carmine in Florence—Scenes from the Life of Peter by Masaccio (1401–1428). Photographic reproduction and original work in the public domain.

It's impossible to talk about the Catholic Church without considering the role of the pope, and for a Roman Catholic it's impossible to talk about the pope without talking about Peter.

I'm a big fan of Peter. He was impulsive, often spoke first before he really thought through the question, and made some mistakes. I am a fan because I can relate. Peter was also the obvious leader of the apostles. He was an amazing man and a great leader, and, like most of the apostles, he was martyred because of his belief in Jesus Christ.

The Catholic Church makes some unique claims regarding Peter, and one of their foundational beliefs is that the pope is a direct successor of Peter and, as a result, is the head of the church.

Let's begin this relatively delicate topic by first examining the Roman Catholic teachings regarding the pope. These would include:

- Christ made Peter the leader and the first pope.
- Christ made Peter the ultimate authority and leader of the church.
- Peter became the first bishop of Rome, making Rome and the bishop of Rome the head of the true church.
- This authority, leadership, and infallibility is passed on to Peter's successors—the popes.

As we begin to discuss this cardinal doctrine of the Roman Catholic Church, I want to be upfront that I have no problem with the pope or his role in leading the largest Christian denomination, the Roman Catholic Church. Churches still need someone or some group that is in charge, someone designated as the leader(s). In industry we have had presidents and chairmen in charge for years and started calling the top guy or gal in business the chief executive officer about twenty-five years ago. Almost all organizations have some formalized procedures to provide for succession (e.g., new CEOs), and large organizations typically have some accountability group (e.g., a board of directors, board of elders, or trustees) that provides oversight.

Many Bible scholars will argue that having accountability through a plurality of elders was the way the church was originally organized. However, we know from history that soon after the death of the original apostles, a single elder or bishop who would be the head of a geographical area and a group of churches replaced the plurality of elders in the church.

Let's take a look at the unique issues related to the role, the authority, and the position of the pope.

Peter as the Leader and in Rome

Peter was certainly one of the leaders of the apostles. He, James, and John are often the three included in the inner circle with Jesus. In every one of the lists of the apostles in the Gospels, Peter is named first. He was present on the Mount of Transfiguration with James and John. Jesus took him along with James and John into the Garden of Gethsemane.

While Peter denied Christ, as Jesus had predicted, Jesus restored him with the "do you love me...feed my sheep" dialogue recorded in John 21:17.

The book of Acts identifies Peter as one of the leaders of the early church. As an apostle he had influence on and was honored by the early church. In the catacombs of Rome, there are inscriptions honoring both Peter and Paul.

However, there are no indications in these inscriptions or in any other historical writings from the first century that Peter exercised any authority in the church in general or in Rome in particular.

We do have some clue regarding early church leadership in the scriptures. Luke, Peter, and Paul all discussed early church leadership. Luke is the author of both the Gospel attributed to him as well as the Acts of the Apostles; the apostle Peter wrote both 1 Peter and 2 Peter; and the apostle Paul wrote nearly one third of the New Testament.

In particular Paul talked about the role of Peter in his letter to the Galatians:

> They recognized that I had been entrusted with the task of preaching the Gospel to the uncircumcised, just as Peter had been to the circumcised. For God, who was at work in Peter as an apostle to the circumcised, was also at work in me as an apostle to the Gentiles. (Gal. 2:7–8)

Paul's journey and arrival in Rome are documented in great detail in the book of Acts, chapter 28. Luke wrote about Paul's welcome to Rome, his imprisonment, and his teachings. Paul was in Rome for two years, and, according to tradition, he was beheaded, which would have been the appropriate manner of capital punishment for a Roman citizen.

By tradition Peter made it to Rome and was crucified upside down. However, there is neither biblical record nor early church writings attesting to Peter's arrival, ministry, or death in Rome.

Peter is not referenced at all in the Acts of the Apostles after the Council of Jerusalem in Acts, chapter 15. In this council Paul and Barnabas traveled to Jerusalem to have the apostles settle the dispute regarding circumcision. After some discussion Peter addressed the issue, and then James, Jesus's brother, provided the final decision.

It is interesting to note that we have extrabiblical evidence (historical writings regarding this time period) that state it was not Peter who was chosen to lead the early church, but James, the brother of the Lord.

Eusebius Pamphilus (AD 263–340) was a bishop and a scholar in the early church. He is best known for his ecclesiastical history, including the history of the church to AD 324. His stated intention in writing the history was to connect the church of which he was part to the beginnings of Christianity.

Eusebius wrote:

> Then there was James who was known as the brother of the Lord. For he too was called Joseph's son, and

Joseph, Christ's father, though in fact the Virgin was his betrothed, and before they came together she was found to be with child by the Holy Spirit, as the inspired Gospel narrative tells us. This James, whom the early Christians surnamed the Righteous because of his outstanding virtue, was the first (as the recorders tell us) to be elected to the episcopal throne of the Jerusalem church.[19]

Eusebius's attribution of James rather than Peter as the first bishop is echoed by another historian of the early church, Clement of Alexandria (AD 150–215), who preceded Eusebius by fifty years. Clement was also a scholar, and both the Roman Catholic Church and the Orthodox Church considered him a church father.

Clement wrote:

James the Righteous, John, and
Peter, James and John, after the Ascension of the Savior, did not claim preeminence because the Savior had especially honored them, but chose James the Righteous as Bishop of Jerusalem...James the Righteous, John, and Peter were entrusted by the Lord after his resurrection with the higher knowledge. They imparted it to the other apostles, and the other apostles to the seventy.[20]

In addition, while we don't typically try to prove something by its omission, despite the fact that Luke recorded that Paul was in Rome for the last years of Paul's life, Luke did not mention Peter's being in Rome. During the time Paul was in Rome, the same two years Luke recorded, Paul wrote to Timothy from Rome around AD 65 and talked about a number of Christians who had served with him, including Demas, Crescens, Luke, and Titus. However, Paul related that he had "fought the good fight" and that the "time of his death was near." In his final words from Rome, he encouraged Timothy to come and visit if possible and that "only Luke is with me" (2 Tim. 4:11).

It's a stretch to find early support of a claim that Peter founded the church in Rome or exercised any authority while there. However, by the fourth century, the tradition of Peter's being the first bishop of Rome was well established, and Pope Leo I used it to request primacy among all of the other bishops.

The Pope's Authority in the Church

For one thousand years, and actually to this day, as evidenced by the Second Vatican Council in 1965, the authority of the church was in the councils. We saw this earlier, when I referenced the Council of Jerusalem in Acts, chapter 15 (it is also recorded in Galatians, chapter 2). According to the account in the Bible, Judas and Silas delivered the apostles' (plural) determination by letter to the churches—not the ruling of one individual. However, had it been one individual, he would most likely have been James, not Peter.

Constantine called the Council of Nicaea in AD 325, later called the First Ecumenical Council because it included various known Christian churches and was presided over by Constantine and the Patriarch of Alexandria. The bishop of Rome (a.k.a. the pope) did not attend this council.

The bishop of Rome attended the Council of Constantinople in AD 381 and the Council of Ephesus in AD 431. The emperors and empresses of Rome called these councils and later councils together, and the decisions were made by majority vote of the bishops in attendance. The bishop of Rome did not have a major role in these councils until the First Lateran Council of 1123, after the Great Schism, when the bishop of Rome excommunicated the bishop of Constantinople, and the other patriarchs of Alexandria, Jerusalem, and Antioch sided with the latter.

Good Popes, Bad Popes

Anyone who has seen the TV series *The Borgias* has seen some of the horrible accusations that have been leveled against the popes. As with most accusations against world leaders, there are both truth and exaggeration in the charges. History records that there have been some great popes and some really bad popes. We aren't going to go through an exhaustive list, as it would be contrary to the overall theme of reconciliation and fairness. However, some examples would be helpful.

Bad popes include Stephen VI (AD 896–897), who had his predecessor exhumed and put on trial. Pope Benedict IX was a highly immoral man who may have been made pontiff when he was in his early teens or possibly as old as twenty. He reportedly sold his papal throne, and later the church excommunicated him. Great popes outnumber these bad popes ten to one, and if I were listing them, there would be many, including the recent John Paul II (now a saint), St. Leo I, and St. Gregory I.

The Honor Versus the Authority of the Pope

As we look back to the early church, and even as late as the medieval Church, the bishop of Rome was definitely in a position of honor. This was recorded specifically in the Edict of Milan in AD 313. There was, however, a clear distinction between honor and authority in many historical documents from the same period. Historically bishops (and patriarchs in particular) had authority over geographical regions. A number of church councils referenced this authority, and clearly it was part of the Roman state governance. Bishops and patriarchs who overstepped their geographic boundaries were often criticized by the others.

Apostolic Succession

The Roman Catholic Church identifies the pope as the successor of St. Peter. Early church writings indicated that all of the bishops were the successors of the apostles, but if particular leadership was truly in the hands of the apostle Peter, there is neither biblical nor historical indication that this leadership was to be passed on to his particular successors.

The actual record of successors in the Bible is not so honorable. After two hundred years of rule by judges, ancient Israel appealed to the prophet Samuel and demanded a king. The biblical account makes it very clear that both the prophet as well as Jehovah God were displeased with the request and predicted Israel would ultimately suffer by having one leader who had great authority and no accountability.

Samuel appointed Saul as king and typically disappointed both God and man. Jonathan was his successor and heir, but God had a better plan and put young David on the throne as the king of Judah and later all of Israel. King David had a number of sons, and before wise King Solomon came to the throne, David's sons Amnon and Daniel were likely successors. Amnon, however, was best known for the rape of his half sister, Tamar, and the Bible doesn't mention Daniel, also called Chileab, other than telling us that his mother was Abigail.

Man's plans to name a successor of a successful or even a great man actually fail much more often than they succeed. I've seen this a number of times in business and industry, as I've had many good friends who were good business leaders, talented entrepreneurs, wise, and very successful. Their sons and daughters, however, were not as talented. Many businesses don't survive when the second or third generation is in power.

Interestingly (at least to me), the only instance of succession in the New Testament is recorded in the book of Acts. After Jesus's ascension, the apostles traveled back to Jerusalem and returned to the upper room. There they decided to replace the traitor, Judas. Peter stood up and used an obscure scripture in the book of Psalms that stated, "May another take his place of leadership" (Ps.109:8).

The apostles nominated two men to succeed Judas as one of the twelve apostles. The apostles prayed and decided to cast lots (equivalent to flipping a coin). Eventually they chose Matthias as the successor.

This is not the place to discuss the role of the Holy Spirit (which had not yet indwelled the apostles), biblical inerrancy, and historical accuracy. However, it is clear that while it was the apostles' intention to put Matthias in a particular role, the apostle Paul was the one the Lord picked. In my church history class, I usually ask my students to name the books of the Bible written by the apostle Matthias, to wake them up to the obvious fact that succession, leadership, calling, and even apostleship are of the Lord's doing and not something either man or process can guarantee.

CHAPTER THIRTEEN

The Saints

Burying St. Joseph Upside Down

Icon of the apostle Paul, fourteenth century, State Museum
of Fine Art—Georgia. Photographic reproduction and
original work in the public domain.

When I attended St. Joseph's Catholic School and became an altar boy, I had never heard of the practice of burying a St. Joseph statue in the ground in order to bring good luck in selling a house. I first heard of the practice much later, in the 1980s, when the real estate market was soft.

If you haven't heard of this practice, let me elaborate. According to some unofficial Catholic websites, the custom supposedly dates back to the sixteenth century. The story goes that St. Teresa of Avila, founder of the Carmelite Order, was building new convents and needed money to purchase land. Her thoughtful nuns called on St. Joseph to help with getting the funding and then also buried medals with St. Joseph's likeness on them. Apparently the process worked, and the custom continued.

Today on Amazon, anxious home sellers can purchase a St. Joseph Home Seller Statue Kit for less than $10.00, with instructions on how to bury a three-inch statue. For some reason the statue is to be buried upside down. Catholic Supply of St. Louis offers four different kits, including a deluxe version for $11.95 and one in Spanish.

The early saints had nothing to do with home sales. However, we do have indications that very early (i.e., the second century) in the history of the church, saints were associated with the miraculous and God's special favor.

Martyr to Saint

The Greek word that is translated as *saint* is *hagios*, and it is found more than two hundred times in the New Testament. It's often translated as "holy," including in "holy ones" and "holy places." When it refers to people (i.e., *saints*) it is always in reference to living, breathing people who are called and closely following God. The only exception to the living and breathing saints is in the book of Revelation, which references saints who have died (been martyred) and those who are praying, either living or dead (i.e., prayers of the saints).

When persecution broke out against the church in the Roman Empire, many Christians were martyred. The original meaning of the word *martyr* was "witness," as these men and women were witnesses of the faith.

In the early church, Paul referred often to the early Christians as saints, even calling himself the "least of all saints" (Eph. 3:8, NKJ). The early martyrs (dead saints) were certainly witnesses of the faith and were honored, just as Jewish tradition had honored the Old Testament patriarchs, prophets, and martyrs.

As the church grew, particularly when it became joined with the state, the tradition and use of the word *saint* obviously changed. Calling a living person a saint, particularly using the Greek *hagios* (meaning "separated" or "consecrated to God"), and using the same word for those who had given their lives either through martyrdom or by great example of their holiness, seemed inappropriate. As a result the word *saint* was reserved exclusively until the time of the Reformation for those who were already dead and had already proven their faithfulness and holiness, often through martyrdom.

During the first few centuries of the church, people began to remember, honor, and even venerate many saints. As time went on, there were a number of unexplained, miraculous, or, at least, fortunate events attributed to requests made or venerations of particular saints.

There was no official process of determining who was a saint until the twelfth century, when a papal bull confirmed the process of canonizing a saint to include the inquiries into their lives and whether miracles were attributed to them. The Roman Catholic Church has canonized more than ten thousand named saints, the vast majority of them within the past one hundred years.

Officially the Roman Catholic Church does not teach that people are to pray *to* the saints but that they are to ask the saints to pray *for* them.

Religious Icons

Saints have also been a very important part of the history of the Eastern Orthodox Church, the origin of which is the same as the Eastern and Western parts of the Catholic Church, which were united until AD

1054. However, in the Eastern Orthodox (or just simply Orthodox) Catholic Church, saints were actually a more important part of the official liturgy and practices.

Images of the saints were a problem in the early church, primarily because of the Second Commandment:

> You shall not make for yourself a graven image, nor a likeness of anything that is in heaven above or on earth below, nor of those things which are in the waters under the earth. You shall not adore them, nor shall you worship them. I am the Lord your God: strong, zealous, visiting the iniquity of the fathers on the sons to the third and fourth generation of those who hate me, and showing mercy to thousands of those who love me and keep my precepts. (Ex. 20:4–6, Catholic Public Domain Version)

Both the East and the West went through periods of time when they used religious images that were later destroyed by those who wanted to purify the church in their attempt to honor the Second Commandment. In the East very clever artists solved the problem by creating icons that were not carved, or graven, but flat, two-dimensional representations or likenesses of events (e.g., parables, the crucifixion), as well as Jesus Christ, the Virgin Mary, angels, and the saints. These two-dimensional images, often painted on wood, are called icons (from the Greek *eikon*, meaning "image").

There were a few very tumultuous times in the church relating to these statues and icons. In the late seventh century, the Muslims who had started a very successful conquest of Christian lands in Africa and the Middle East moved against the Byzantium (Roman) Empire. Roman Emperor Leo III, who sat on his throne in Constantinople, began to listen to some of the religious leaders who said the Muslims were successful because they did not make images of God while the Christians had numerous icons. Many religious leaders believed that icons were sacrilegious and that religious pictures, icons, and relics had no place in Christian worship services.

Around AD 730 Emperor Leo III ordered the removal of the icons of Christ that were prevalent over altars, to be replaced by a simple cross. The people who were in favor of removing and often destroying the icons were called iconoclasts (meaning "image breakers"). Many religious leaders and laypeople resisted the emperor's orders, which ultimately led to mobs, riots, and bloodshed; both religious and Byzantine leaders dispatched soldiers and even armies.

More than 330 bishops attended the Seventh Ecumenical Council, convened by Emperor Constantine V in AD 754. The council ruled in favor of the iconoclasts and ultimately forbade the painting of the forms of saints and declared the use anathema, or condemned. However, this council was also called the Robber Council, as most of the patriarchs did not attend. The Second Council of Nicaea overturned its ruling in AD 787.

The use of graven images or painted pictures of saints as well as the veneration of the saints was a major issue again in the sixteenth century, during the Protestant Reformation. Praying to the saints and attributing to them qualities that God alone possesses was a great concern to the reformers of the time. Some of the Protestant reformers encouraged the removal of these images in order to return the church to what they considered a more appropriate understanding of prayer and intercession. They embraced a broader definition of idolatry that included the veneration, prayers, and worship of the saints.

Unfortunately some of these reformers who favored removal of statues and images of saints, like the iconoclasts centuries earlier, too often found it expedient to destroy centuries of art in painting, frescoes, and statues.

CHAPTER FOURTEEN

The Virgin Mary

The Four Marian Dogmas

Mother and Child by Giovanni Bellini, oil on panel, circa 1465. Location: Kimbell Art Museum, Fort Worth, Texas. Photographic reproduction and original work in the public domain.

There are entire books dedicated to the topic of the Virgin Mary. There is likely no other topic that can create such an emotional response from both proponents of as well as detractors from her roles in both history and faith. However, that is exactly why we need to take some time to discuss the teachings of the Roman Catholic Church related to the Virgin Mary and attempt to find some common understanding and appreciation of these matters of faith.

One of the first things I would like to establish is that belief in the Virgin Birth of Jesus Christ is a universal church teaching regardless of denomination or sect, East or West, Protestant, Catholic, Pentecostal, Evangelical, or non-denominational. Since my parents didn't fully understand this, I assume that many Roman Catholics probably misunderstand that while the role of the Virgin Mary is different for those who are not Roman Catholic or Orthodox, it does not mean some Christian churches do not believe in the Virgin Birth.

The Virgin Birth is an essential part of our faith and was cemented in the fourth century, in the Nicene Creed. In addition many non-Catholics, including me, have a great respect and reverence for the Virgin Mary despite some differences regarding the belief in the ongoing ministry of the Virgin Mary.

My introduction to Roman Catholic teachings on the Virgin Mary came from my early years at St. Joseph's Catholic School under the Dominican nuns. Most if not all of them took Mary as one of their names (e.g., Sister Mary Dominick, Sister Mary Angelina, Sister Mary Luke, Sister Mary Annunciata, etc.). While the nuns never told us the particular reason, their strong devotion to the Virgin Mary was obvious. From their names to the large rosaries wrapped around their waists to their habits that resembled many medieval pictures and statues of the Virgin Mary, their devotion was clear, constant, and pure. Despite the negative stories, movies, and Broadway musicals, the nuns at my school were great educators. In addition they were great examples of chastity and holiness. They never hit us with their rosary beads and generally were in good spirits, except when discipline was needed and their enforcer training took over.

St. Dominick founded the Dominican nuns in AD 1206, reportedly after his missionary trip to Albi in Southern France. Albi was the headquarters of a religious sect known as the Albigensians, also known as the Cathars, which had grown in influence and numbers. This religious sect was highly influential in Southern France, and Pope Innocent III judged it to be heretical and outside of the main teachings of the Catholic Church. While the Albigensians definitely embraced some heretical beliefs, their spiritual practices included a very simple lifestyle, zealous preaching, and humility. They were no friends of Rome, considering the pope a mere man and the beast of Babylon. These Albigensians, or Cathars, were ultimately eliminated along with many other Christians, including many loyal Catholics and Waldensians (very devoted Christians and followers of Peter Waldo) through a bloody, twenty-year period often called the Albigensian Crusade.

St. Dominick was more interested in the spiritual conversion of the Albigensian men and women than killing them, as was the primary design of the crusade. While Dominick achieved only limited success, he ultimately became the protector and spiritual father to several Albigensian women. These women had embraced an ascetic lifestyle that ultimately became the foundation for the Dominican nuns. If the date of their formation is correct (AD 1206), that means the Dominican nuns preceded the Dominican Friars by a decade.

Through the teachings of these Dominican nuns, we young students at St. Joseph's were introduced to various beliefs regarding the Virgin Mary. Some of these teachings were doctrine approved by the Catholic Church, and others were simply traditions. While widespread, these unofficial practices and beliefs often were little more than wishful thinking and folklore.

There are four official Catholic doctrines related to the Virgin Mary, often referred to as the Four Marian Dogmas. These are:

1) Mary as the Mother of God.
2) The Immaculate Conception.
3) The Perpetual Virginity of Mary.
4) The Assumption of Mary.

While some of these dogmas are relatively recent official additions, their formation, belief, and acceptance go back centuries, with the oldest going back to the Council of Ephesus (AD 431). Each has an interesting and highly documented history. We'll address each one briefly, going from the oldest to the newest.

Mary as the Mother of God

All Christian churches teach that Jesus was conceived of the Holy Spirit and born of the Virgin Mary. As a result Mary is the mother of Christ—the mother of Jesus, the Son of God. As we also believe that Jesus is God, the second part of the Trinity (Father, Son, and Holy Spirit), we can infer that Mary is therefore the mother of God.

This reasoning was hotly contested in the fifth century. By that time the veneration of the saints as well as the Virgin Mary was common, and the Virgin Mary had a position of high honor (Latin: *hyperdulia*) in the church. However, at the time, there was also a controversy centered on the teachings of the archbishop of Constantinople, Nestorius, who argued that Mary's title in her role regarding the birth of Jesus should be *Christotokos* (Greek: Χριστοτόκος, "Christ bearer") rather than *Theotokos* (Greek: Θεοτόκος, "God bearer").

Theological terms are often debated and their definitions overly complicated, as if to baffle rather than clarify. But for the scholar, there are serious implications in the different terms. Nestorius argued that Jesus had two natures, one divine and one human, and in the incarnation the God-man became man.

The Nestorian issue was addressed at the Councils of Ephesus (AD 431) and Chalcedon (AD 451), and the terms Theotokos and/or Mother of God were officially attributed to the Virgin Mary. While this title had more to do with the nature of Jesus Christ, it was a huge win for those in the church who were, at the time, embracing more of the mystical traditions of the Virgin Mary. Interestingly, much of the then-popular folklore about Mary, including how angels had attended to her after the crucifixion, how John and the Apostles were transported to her side, and how she was able to perform miracles and answer prayers, were part of

74

an apocryphal book called *Transitus Maria*.[21] The pope condemned this book in AD 500, but many of the stories survived and became part of the determination for some of the other Roman Catholic doctrines regarding the Virgin Mary.

Immaculate Conception

The second of these doctrines is the Immaculate Conception. This Catholic doctrine embraces the teaching that from the moment of her conception, the Virgin Mary was preserved from original sin. The Catholic Church has taught since the fourth century that the sin of Adam was passed on to all succeeding generations and represented the original sin of mankind that was removed through baptism. As God picked the Virgin Mary to be the mother of the Christ child, she was preserved from the stain (Latin: *macula*) of original sin. Further, as Mary was declared full of grace by the angel Gabriel, this condition was a declaration of what was, not what would be.

Many people misunderstand this dogma of the Roman Catholic Church. This teaching does not refer to Jesus's conception, which, according to scripture and accepted by all Christians, was through the power of the Holy Spirit. Nor does this teaching indicate that Mary remained sinless. Catholics often get this wrong and defend the Virgin Mary as the sinless one when the dogma and official teaching refer only to original sin, not all sin. However, as the sin of Adam also refers to the predilection of all men to be sinners, it would have been a natural assumption, perhaps intentional, that Mary actually remained sinless.

The official declaration of the doctrine of the Immaculate Conception didn't come until December 8, 1854, when Pope Pius IX declared (and I paraphrase) that the Virgin Mary was conceived in the first instant of her conception by a unique, singular grace and privilege of Almighty God in view of the merits of Jesus Christ, the Savior of the human race, and she was therefore preserved exempt from all stain of original sin.[22] Many non-Catholic observers have suggested this declaration was a test balloon and preamble to the doctrine of the infallibility of the pope that the first Vatican Council ratified in 1870.

The Perpetual Virginity of Mary

One of the more historically and culturally interesting doctrines regarding the Virgin Mary—one that Roman Catholics and the Eastern Orthodox accept almost universally, though other Christians reject it— is the Perpetual Virginity of Mary, the mother of Jesus. For many who attend my classes on Roman Catholic theology and the history of the church, this is the one dogma, the one teaching of the Catholic Church that leads to the most discussion and dialogue.

From the Roman Catholic perspective, the perpetual virginity of Mary is so integral to the mystique and veneration of Mary, it goes unchallenged. Virgin is not a first name but a condition, and if she is called the Virgin Mary, it's not because she once was but because she always was and always will be.

Most Protestants are not even aware that this would be part of the Roman Catholic doctrine regarding the Virgin Mary. The belief in Jesus's being conceived while Mary was still a virgin is nearly universally accepted and unquestioned. However, even a casual reading of the New Testament provides references to a mother and father, a man and wife, who lived together and raised their children. Further multiple references to the family include references to brothers and sisters of Jesus and no further explanation of an extended family or previous marriage.

However, Catholic and Orthodox scholars argue that some of these references to brothers and sisters of Jesus could actually have referred to an extended family or cousins. In addition, at the time of the Protestant Reformation, the belief in the perpetual virginity of the Virgin Mary was so universally accepted that both Martin Luther of Germany and John Calvin, the French reformer and great theologian, not only believed in it but were defenders of it as well.

Mary's perpetual virginity versus her ultimate sexual union with her husband, Joseph, may be debated but has little if any impact on the more important doctrines and teachings of the church. Let it be said we may agree to disagree.

The Assumption of Mary

The official doctrine of the Assumption of Mary is very recent, added only in 1950 by Pope Pius XII. However, Pope Leo IV was known to have permitted an annual feast celebrating her assumption as early as the eighth century. Church historians agree that there is nothing written in either the biblical or other historical records regarding Mary's demise, departure, death, or assumption.

Apparently the ancient church identified two different locations of Mary's grave. There are historical records indicating early Christian pilgrimages to Mary's burial site in the Kidron Valley, near Jerusalem, and the ancient city of Ephesus—locations that are more than 1,100 miles apart.

While Eastern (Orthodox) and Western (Roman Catholic) teachings regarding Mary are similar, the Eastern Orthodox teaching is that the Virgin Mary died and was resurrected three days later. The Roman Catholic teaching is interesting, as while many teach the Virgin Mary was assumed directly into heaven, the official teaching of the church prior to 1950 was that she died and then was received later both body and soul.

While the Western church didn't necessarily teach about a three-day interval, Pope Pius XII's proclamation avoided the subject altogether and simply declared that "the Immaculate Mother of God, the ever Virgin Mary, having completed the course of her earthly life, was assumed body and soul into heavenly glory."[23]

Since the time of the Reformation, most non-Roman Catholic Churches and denominations have not tried to encourage overtly or suppress the teaching of the Assumption of the Virgin Mary. Catholic theologians agree there is no biblical support of the doctrine, but sacred tradition embraces it. Many non–Roman Catholic theologians, having no biblical evidence to support the doctrine, don't believe it to be helpful theology.

CHAPTER FIFTEEN

Rosary Beads

Glory Be

A Catholic rosary with a St. Benedict medal placed in
the center of the cross. Photographic reproduction and
original work in the public domain.

Roaming Catholics

S t. Joseph's Catholic School occupied two floors of an original church building that was built in 1907. In the mid-1960s my brother and I were crowded into classes that occupied not only these two floors but also the basement. Four additional classes were held temporarily in a metal double-wide trailer until the faithful in the church could raise the funds to build a permanent addition.

The school addition opened when I was in fifth grade, and for the first time we had the equivalent of a café, a gym, and an auditorium. Of course these three were all just one room and no larger than any one of the names would imply, but to the priests and nuns of St. Joseph's church and school, they were their pride and joy.

Sister Mary Dominick was my fifth-grade teacher and one of the younger nuns. While all of the nuns wore the traditional black-and-white, head-to-toe habits of the Dominican order, some would occasionally wear different shoes. In the winter, boots were more functional than the traditional shapeless and uncomfortable-looking black shoes that were the standard footwear of choice. Sister Mary Dominick, however, preferred Jeepers. For those of you who were not familiar with this inexpensive brand of athletic shoes sold at Sears, Jeepers were popular because they looked very much like the high-top Converse basketball shoes but were less expensive. They came in both low and high tops and in both boys' and girls' sizes. Because they were less expensive than Converse, Keds, or PF Flyers, Jeepers were often called "cheaper Jeepers."

We kids liked that Sister Mary Dominick wore Jeepers and loved it when she played kickball with us, often kicking the ball farther than many of us boys.

One of the popular Catholic movies of the day was *Miracle of Our Lady of Fatima*, which had been released for more than ten years and had actually been on TV a few times. Sister Mary Dominick had a sixteen-millimeter version of the film, and one Friday afternoon all of us sat cross-legged on the floor of the new café-gym-atorium to watch it.

The film was based on an event that took place in 1917 in Fatima, Portugal. Three shepherd children prayed the rosary while watching their sheep, and to their amazement they encountered an angel and then, a little later, saw a vision of the Virgin Mary in a cloud. While most people were skeptical, including their parents and some of the local village priests, the children insisted they not only saw the Virgin Mary but that she gave them messages of peace and hope. The Virgin Mary provided a date when she would show visions so people would believe her message. The movie ended with the 1960s version of special effects—the recreation of a spectacular event that is officially recorded as a miracle by the Roman Catholic Church. While many accounts vary, most record that the sun danced in the sky for a period of about ten minutes.

One of the themes that seemed obvious to me in the movie, and I was only about eleven at the time, was that the rosary was an important part of the religion of these shepherd children. One of the children couldn't see the vision at first and had to pray the rosary harder in order to be worthy to see the vision. The rosary was also something we saw daily on our teachers, as the nuns wore the rosary around their waists.

Millions of Catholics use the rosary, and its introduction is often attributed to St. Dominick, who, in 1214, according to many accounts, saw an apparition of the Virgin Mary. She was said to have spoken to him and told him the key to his success in ministry would be to teach the people how to say the rosary. The legend connected with the rosary recounts that St. Dominick took the Virgin Mary's advice to heart and from that time forward preached the rosary—so much so that when he founded the Dominican order of preachers as well as the Dominican order of nuns, they too were dedicated to both the Virgin Mary as well as the rosary.

The typical rosary the Western Roman Catholic Church uses consists of five decades (five tens) that begin with the Our Father (also known as the Lord's Prayer to non-Catholics) and then ten Hail Marys followed by a Glory Be.

If you count the number of beads and the prayers, there are seven Our Fathers, six Glory Bes, and fifty-six Hail Marys on the modern rosary. However, its history and development are interesting and can be controversial for those who have a strong devotion to both the Virgin Mary and the rosary.

Based on most of the historical research, the development of the practice of using beads in prayer has a very significant connection to the practice of the early monks in their Liturgy of the Hours, which began with the early Christian ascetics and hermits of the third and fourth centuries. These holy men desired to separate themselves completely from the vices and temptations of society as well as some of the corruption that was creeping into the church, and they developed strict disciplines to keep their minds and bodies focused on spiritual things. The Liturgy of the Hours (the equivalent of the Office, which is the required obligation of every Roman Catholic cleric to pray through daily) originally included reading through the 150 Psalms. These were broken into fifteen decades of ten psalms that would be recited or prayed at various prescribed times during the day. These daily readings were a condensed version of the entire Liturgy of the Hours and were often called the breviary (from the Latin *brevis*, meaning "short or concise").

By the Middle Ages, or the medieval period, in Europe (roughly from the fall of Rome in the fifth century until the Renaissance, beginning in Italy in the fifteenth century), the spiritual lives of the monks and priests and many of those in the religious orders fully embraced the fifteen decades of prayers, which were often shortened to five, repeated three times during the day.

The common people thought very highly of the monks and other religious ascetics, and many of the people came to the monks to help them learn how to pray. Since most of the common people were illiterate, the monks taught them a few prayers they could easily memorize and then repeat often during the day. History records that some of these early prayers included the Our Father (Latin: *Paternoster*), which the people often chanted in Latin despite the fact that by that time most didn't understand it.

Over a period of time, the custom even among the monks was to tie 150 knots on a cord and use them to keep track of their chants of the Paternoster. For those who could not read Latin, these 150 chants became known as the poor man's Breviary and was most likely the Christian origin of the modern-day rosary. By the fourteenth century,

groups of Christians who had a deep devotion to the Virgin Mary modified the poor man's Breviary into five decades of Hail Marys rather than
the Our Fathers.

All of this is a great story tracing the history of the rosary and may be
completely factual. However, most historians, including Catholic historians, are not able to connect any reference by St. Dominick to the rosary.
In fact the Nine Ways of Prayer of St. Dominick that were attributed to
him, just after his death, mention neither the rosary nor the Virgin Mary.

The official encyclopedia of the Catholic Church, *New Advent*, comes
to a similar conclusion:

> [We] possess hundreds, even thousands, of manuscripts
> containing devotional treatises, sermons, chronicles,
> Saints' lives, etc., written by the (Dominican) preachers
> between 1220 and 1450; but no single verifiable passage
> has yet been produced which speaks of the Rosary as
> instituted by St. Dominick or which even makes much
> of the devotion as one specially dear to his children. The
> charters and other deeds of the Dominican convents for
> men and women...are equally silent. Neither do we find
> any suggestion of a connection between St. Dominick
> and the Rosary in the paintings and sculptures of these
> two and a half centuries. Even the tomb of St. Dominick
> at Bologna and the numberless frescoes representing the
> brethren of his order ignore the Rosary completely.[24]

According to many Protestants and detractors of the rosary, the rosary
encourages both vain repetitions in prayer as well as prayers directed
to the Virgin Mary, a practice the reformers in the sixteenth century
discouraged. Some claim the history of the rosary is closely related to
the development of the Muslim Tisphi, or worry beads, that have been
popular since the ascent of Islam in the seventh century. According to
Islam the Tisphi contains thirty-three beads that are used three times for
a total of ninety-nine, which equates to the "beautiful names of Allah."

Male Christians in the Middle East adopted the same practice, using the thirty-three beads to represent the thirty-three years of the earthly ministry of Jesus Christ and repeated the beads three times, representing the three members of the Trinity.

However, my independent research indicates that many religious cultures, including Christian, Islam, and Hindu, used beads at various times to assist in their prayers and devotion. It would be natural that Christians under the rule of Islam would modify cultural patterns to fit their beliefs more closely.

Many adherents of the rosary claim a conclusion regarding the connection between St. Dominick and the Virgin Mary and the rosary cannot be dismissed because of the absence of literary evidence (in the study of logic, an inference referred to as an argument from ignorance). Many of the faithful devotees of the rosary claim that Marian apparitions, healings, and answers to prayers can be attributed to praying the rosary and encourage its use. As a closing comment, many of the Catholic popes, including most of the recent ones, have also championed the rosary.

CHAPTER SIXTEEN

The Bible

No Wite-Out Allowed

Oxyrhynchus Papyri, discovered by Grenfel and Hunt, circa
1900, of the Old Testament book Amos 2, written circa
750 BC. Copied by a scribe circa AD 550. Photographic
reproduction and original work in the public domain.

We found out just before school started that the rumor we had heard was true: Sister Mary Ann, our principal for the past few years, was also going to be our seventh-grade teacher. She would teach our combined class of more than fifty students. We had been split in both fifth and sixth grades but ended up back together in one large class. Discipline was never an issue at St. Joseph's Catholic School, as from the first grade we had learned that the nuns were not kidding around when they wanted us to be quiet, sit down, stand up, or line up.

Most of the parents were pleased with Sister Mary Ann as the principal. She had a pleasant smile, seemed to remember the names of most of the students and their parents, and had kept the tuition low. As a teacher, however, she seemed really to excel.

Early in the school year, she seemed disappointed that while most of us had been in a Catholic school for the past six years, few of us seemed to be leaning toward Catholic vocations (the priesthood, becoming a brother, or a nun).

As a result she dedicated some money, and all of us fifty-plus students started receiving subscriptions to *Maryknoll Magazine*. Each month there were articles about missionary activities in places such as South America and Africa, human-interest stories on the lives of priests or nuns, and other stories she would then talk about in class.

She also obtained for us our own copies of an illustrated edition of the New Testament of the New American Bible. Sister Mary Ann was disappointed by the lack of Bible understanding in the majority of the class, and I was definitely in the unlearned majority.

She taught us how to look up Bible verses by book, chapter, and verse, so we could easily reference Jesus's very often-quoted saying "And I tell you that you are Peter, and on this rock I will build my church." She told us that we could find that in Matthew 16:18.

I recently saw my illustrated St. Joseph's edition of the New Testament at my parents' home. It is almost embarrassing to admit how little use it had. However, I've learned to love the Bible and since that time have become better schooled in its use and its history.

The Bible has two divisions: the Old Testament and the New Testament. The Old Testament includes thirty-nine books. The Catholic editions have forty-six due to the seven additional deuterocanonical (meaning "second-cannon") books, also known as the apocrypha (a Greek word meaning "hidden"). These additional books are omitted from both the Jewish Bible, known as the Mikra or Tanakh, and all current non-Catholic editions.

The Old Testament is further divided into five different categories: the Pentateuch (a word meaning "five"); the historical books, which include information on the kings and the people of Israel and Judah; the poetic books, including the Psalms and Proverbs; and finally what is referred to as the Prophets.

The thirty-nine books we know as the Old Testament were written from approximately 1500 BC (the time of Moses) to around 400 BC, when Nehemiah returned to Jerusalem after the Babylonians' captivity of the Jews.

We have no original copies of the Old Testament as it was originally written on papyrus, a paperlike product made from a plant. Today museums and libraries around the world keep two-thousand-year-old papyrus fragments. They have found that placing the papyrus fragments between two pieces of glass and sealing the edges so they are airtight protects the fragments from further decay.

Papyrus, like parchment, is an organic material and is highly subject to decay. Under the right conditions (i.e., very dry climate and very little air circulation), it holds up surprisingly well. That is exactly why very old papyrus that was sealed in clay pots has been found in desert regions. These amazing discoveries contributed greatly to both the authenticity as well as the historicity of the Bible.

Despite the fact we have no original autographs or ancient copies, we know a lot about the practices of the Jewish scholars who transcribed and made copies of their scriptures. A group of fifth-century AD Jewish scribes and scholars known as the Masoretes perfected the ancient tradition of transcribing the Old Testament texts by carefully counting every letter per line and the total number of the times each Hebrew letter was used (i.e., counting the As, Bs, Cs, or the *alefs, bets, gimels* in Hebrew) in the document; finally they would identify the middle character of the middle line to be sure it was exactly the same. If there was a mistake during the process, the entire page had to be destroyed. There was no Wite-Out allowed.

Because there was so much care in transcribing these ancient documents, we have great confidence that the wording we have today is very, very close to the original.

Dead Sea Scrolls

Three Bedouin shepherds discovered some very ancient scrolls inside clay jars in caves on the West Bank of Israel, very near the Dead Sea, in November 1946. These scrolls eventually found their way to scholars and religious leaders and were found to include the earliest copy of the book of Isaiah. Over a number of years, interrupted briefly by the 1948 Arab-Israeli War, archaeologists and scholars collected a total of 972 manuscripts in a total of eleven caves.

Archaeologists looking at cultural clues in the caves and scientists using carbon dating agreed the scrolls date as early as the third century BC to the first century AD. These 972 manuscripts and tens of thousands of fragments contain copies of every Old Testament book with the exception of the book of Esther.

These Old Testament verses were found to be nearly identical with the Masoretic texts from manuscripts dated to around AD 953. Over the centuries the integrity of the scriptures was preserved. A famous Hebrew scholar, Millar Burrows, wrote, "It is a matter of wonder that through something like one thousand years the text underwent so little alteration."[25]

New Testament Reliability

People who study the historical reliability of the scriptures agree there are more than 5,600 ancient (but not original) Greek New Testament manuscripts and an additional 19,000 ancient manuscripts of the New Testament in Syriac, Latin, Coptic, and various Aramaic languages.

The New Testament compares very favorably and is literally in a completely different class of historically verified manuscripts when compared to classical and generally assumed to be authentic copies of the works of Plato or Aristotle. For example, *The Republic* is universally attributed to Plato, who lived from 427 to 347 BC, and the earliest copy of the work is from AD 900—an approximate time span between the original and earliest copy of about twelve hundred years. In comparison the New Testament is generally assumed to have been written between AD 50 and AD 90, and the earliest copy we have is the Ryland's Papyrus (P52), dated to around AD 150, fewer than one hundred years after the original autograph.

One of the most persuasive arguments for the reliability of the New Testament actually comes not from what it says but what it doesn't say, as a major historical event is obvious by its omission.

In AD 70 a Roman general and future emperor, Titus, destroyed Jerusalem. The destruction was devastating, and most scholars say it was in fulfillment of what Jesus had prophesied just forty years prior. Not one stone was left on top of another, just as Jesus had predicted in Mark 13:2. The historian Josephus documented the destruction in great detail and even wrote that more than one million people were killed, the vast majority of them Jews.[26]

The New Testament often references both the temple and Jerusalem. The temple in Jerusalem is referenced 106 times, and Jerusalem specifically is referenced 141 times, but none of these tells of its destruction. As I mentioned, that the New Testament does not mention this historical and cataclysmic event despite the fact that the majority of the authors of the New Testament were Jewish and writing to primarily a Jewish audience dates the writing of the New Testament to a time prior to AD 70.

This places the writing of the New Testament within thirty to forty years after most of the events reported and the letters, Gospels, and history were circulated. This is a time when it would have been very easy to dispute any inaccuracies or errors.

Look at it this way: Imagine a book about New York City and the World Trade Center with no reference to 9/11. The only conclusion would be that the book was written before September 2001. In the same manner, we can conclude the New Testament was written prior to AD 70, and that provides a great testimony to the historical accuracy of the New Testament.

I am confident the vast majority of the Bible scholars are correct. We can read the Bible today knowing the words have been preserved for us through the centuries, and we should have no doubt of the historical accuracy or the purported authors.

CHAPTER SEVENTEEN

The Sacraments

The Origins of Our Easter Duty

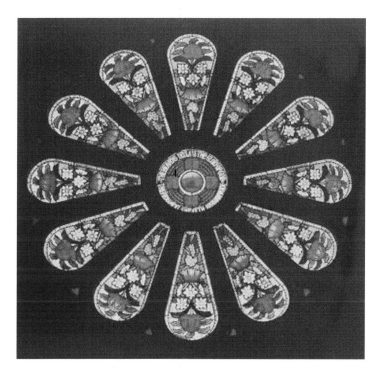

"The heavens declare the glory of God. The firmament showeth his handiwork." Stained glass window in Sydney, St Bede's church. Window is by Alfred Handel in 1932. Photographic reproduction and original work in the public domain.

Roaming Catholics

Within a few months, Sister Mary Ann, our principal and seventh-grade teacher at St. Joseph's, had figured out which of us boys were to be on her lists. She had two: one was the bad list, which included a number of the older boys in sixth, seventh, and eighth grades who could be troublemakers. Looking back I have to smile, as most of the trouble we got into in Catholic school back in the late 1960s was for chewing gum, talking in class when we needed to be quiet, and playing pranks on teachers and students alike.

Rubber bands were my biggest vice, as I found they not only were good for their intended purposes but could travel twenty to thirty feet and, with a little practice, hit an intended target with significant accuracy. I remember being amused that I found the larger, stronger, and best rubber bands in the local supermarket, with the school supplies.

While I was undoubtedly on this troublemaker list from time to time, Sister Mary Ann also invited a few of us who were obviously on a different list to a special after-school activity called Young Catholic Students, or just YCS.

My first YCS meeting was in a local Knights of Columbus hall. I had been there a few times with my dad on Fridays during Lent, as they had their weekly fish fry with French fries and a soda for only two dollars.

At the meeting my friend Steve Zins and I found a couple of other new boys and were surprised to see we were probably the youngest students there. We soon found out that YCS was really targeted to high school students, but Sister Mary Ann had specifically told us about the meeting, as had the local parish priest, Father John.

One of the upcoming events that sounded like fun was a Friday open house at Quigley Preparatory Seminary South, about a month from then. Preparatory seminaries were for boys only and were known for their strict dress codes. Boys were required to wear white shirts and ties. The Quigley blue blazers had the school team's name, the Spartans, on the pocket. Steve and I both signed up for the open house and picked up permission slips to stay overnight in the boys' dorm.

Preparatory seminaries were for all Catholic boys who desired—or whose parents desired for them—to become priests. The high-school education at these seminaries was top-notch, and while there was tuition, it was relatively affordable.

In the United States, most of the preparatory seminaries have closed. The school where Steve Zins and I attended the open house and played in the indoor swimming pool closed in 1989 but had educated four men who became bishops in the thirty years of its existence.

Unfortunately the number of priests in the United States has declined significantly, leaving many parishes without one. In 1965, 1,575 new priests were ordained in the United States; by 2002, the number of newly ordained was only 450. Since the mid-1970s, two thirds of all Catholic seminaries in the United States have closed.[27]

The priesthood is a very important and very central doctrinal distinction in the Roman Catholic Church because only the priest can administer five of the seven sacraments of the church. While there has been a rebirth of the office of deacon in the Catholic Church, deacons aren't priests. Deacons can only baptize (the official teachings of the Catholic Church permit anyone to baptize), and because they are clerics they can officiate in marriage ceremonies.

History records that the early church practiced three sacraments: baptism, the Agape feast, and the Eucharist. When baptism became something administered to an infant, this rite of initiation split into distinct sacraments: baptism shortly after birth and then Confirmation.

Most theologians trace the Agape feast to weekly communal meals that originated during the time of the apostles. St. Paul addressed the problems with these communal meals, which included the Lord's Supper, in his letter to the Corinthians (1 Cor. 11:17–34). St. Jude, one of the twelve apostles, also called Thaddeus, as well as the apostle Peter mentioned these feasts but always in the negative, not because of their intention but because of their attendees. Because of the issues related to these meals (think church potlucks with lots of wine), there is no further reference to Agape feasts by the fourth century.

Theologians and church historians can show that within the first few centuries, the general teaching of the church became rather severe, portraying God as being rather vengeful and those in the church as sinners deserving of hellfire. As a result most participants refused to take Communion, fearing they would do so in an unworthy manner. By the fourth century, the Lord's Supper, or Communion, was taken by the celebrant (priest) only.

We'll talk more about Communion and the Eucharist in later chapters. However, I can mention that for centuries it was rare for the common people to partake of Communion. It was so uncommon that church canon law written in Latin in the twelfth century required the people to partake of the Eucharist annually. This, combined with a Lent requirement to fast and pray, introduced what we know as the Easter duty. The people would prepare themselves during Lent and believed they became worthy enough to receive Communion typically around Easter.

The seven sacraments are:

- Baptism (as infants or adults)
- Eucharist (the Lord's Supper, or Communion)
- Reconciliation (Penance or Confession)
- Confirmation
- Marriage
- Holy Orders
- Anointing of the Sick (Extreme Unction or Last Rites)

Penance (Confession) was introduced in the church over a number of centuries. We have writings from the early fourth century that show the bishop encouraged the penitent to wear sackcloth, sit in ashes, and shave his or her head. The Council of Toledo (AD 589) prescribed the sacrament of Penance to be unrepeatable. As a result penance was considered a once-in-a-lifetime opportunity and typically not received until very late in life.

However, in the thirteenth century, the Fourth Lateran Council required that everyone receive the sacrament of Penance annually (referenced above, in connection with receiving the Eucharist; this was the beginning of what we now know as the Easter duty).

Marriage, Holy Orders, and Extreme Unction (initially identified as Communion for those on their deathbeds) were listed as part of the seven sacraments at the Council of Verona in 1184.

CHAPTER EIGHTEEN

Purgatory

Dust on the Chalkboard

Detail of artist's rendition of purgatory. Source:
Waldburg-Gebetbuch, Stuttgart, circa 1476. Photographic
reproduction and original work in the public domain.

S t. Joseph's Catholic School didn't have any pictures, frescoes, or paintings of purgatory. However, even without pictures like the one above, this hellish place was a frequent topic of conversation. I think I was probably in second or third grade when the nun pointed to a chalkboard that had been used and erased. She pointed to the chalky residue on the green-colored slate. She explained that just as the chalk had been erased, and the chalk dust remained, so when the priests forgive our sins at confession, the sin residue remains, and we must remove it before we can get into heaven.

The priests' and nuns' teachings on purgatory were simple and straightforward: only really good and holy people could go to heaven, and we boys and girls (as well as our moms and dads) were bad and not good or holy enough to go directly to heaven.

Purgatory was the place that dead Catholics went to have the rest of their sins burned off. That may take a really long time, but there were some things people could do while still on earth to take off some of the time. If we didn't do these things, we could spend hundreds or thousands of years in purgatory. The good news, however, was that the only exit door was to heaven.

Through the Flames...

The official Roman Catholic teaching regarding purgatory is rooted in historical Jewish prayers for the dead. History records that as early as the second and third centuries, Christians often made reference to prayers for the departed. The argument that Catholics, therefore, have historically given for purgatory is "why pray for the dead if there isn't some benefit in the prayers?"

One of the common scriptures used in connection with this doctrine is from Paul's first letter to the Corinthians, chapter three, verse fifteen: "If it is burned up, the builder will suffer loss but yet will be saved—even though only as one escaping through the flames."

It was St. Augustine of Hippo (AD 354–450) who first used the term *purgare* in referring to the need for the departed to be purged or cleansed of their sin. While the idea that the Christian departed may still need to be cleansed from their sin was ancient, a place called purgatory was most likely brought into common knowledge by the fourteenth century Italian poet Dante, who wrote of the seven terraces of Mount Purgatory in the epic *Divine Comedy*.

Unlike the more modern Roman Catholic teaching regarding purgatory, in the late Middle Ages it was portrayed as a horrible place of torment, punishment, hellfire, despair, and anguish. It became a popular teaching of the church at that time that indulgences would be granted for individuals who were alive as well as those who had died. These indulgences ranged from simple prayers and good works to gifts of money and property. People who gave substantially to build churches and monasteries would receive years of indulgences that could benefit them or departed relatives suffering in purgatory.

During the Crusades those who took up the sword against the Muslim invaders of Europe or the Holy Land were able to receive plenary, or full, indulgences. There was even an opportunity for knights to receive indulgences that not only provided relief in the afterlife but also allowed them to eat meat on Fridays.[28]

By the time of the Reformation, the sale of indulgences had become a major financial boon for the Catholic Church, and a German monk by the name of Johann Tetzel was charged with the task of raising money for the rebuilding of St. Peter's in Rome. Martin Luther saw the selling of indulgences as not only nonbiblical but another obvious example of the corruption in the Catholic Church, which included the office of the pope. Martin Luther made Johann Tetzel famous—or infamous— because of Tetzel's nondisputed quote: "As soon as the gold in the casket rings; the rescued soul to heaven springs."[29]

Today the Roman Catholic Church continues to embrace both purgatory as well as indulgences. However, since the time of the Reformation, when Martin Luther and others strongly objected to the obvious abuses in the church, including the sale of indulgences, the Roman Catholic Church has modified its teachings so that purgatory is not so frightening. It is not thought to be a place of torment but rather a holding place where venial sins or minor transgressions are purged primarily through time as well as by the prayers of others and through the sacrifice of the altar, meaning the saying of a Mass for the departed. The Catholic Church denies that indulgences were ever sold. It claims people thought they were buying the indulgence where in fact they were just making financial contributions, and the church was providing the spiritual merit from their treasury of merit.

While this chapter is specifically about purgatory and indulgences, the topic of limbo is closely related, so we can spend a little time talking about the history of this teaching as well as the official Roman Catholic teaching, which may be surprising to some.

The nuns at St. Joseph's Catholic School mentioned limbo as well as purgatory. They were obviously two different places in their thinking.

Purgatory was said to be the place for adults who died who had been baptized but had been sinners and needed to be purified before entering heaven. Limbo, on the other hand, was the place where babies and small children who had not been baptized would go. They were stuck somewhere in between Earth and heaven.

In Luke 16:22 Jesus mentioned the Bosom of Abraham in His account of Lazarus and the rich man: "The time came when the beggar died and the angels carried him to Abraham's side. The rich man also died and was buried."

This was the only time Jesus mentioned Abraham's Bosom, and it is not mentioned anywhere else in the Bible. However, in Jewish literature, the afterlife, or the abode of those who died, had a number of different names, and theologians would speculate and teach as with great authority the various places and conditions. The names included the Bosom of Abraham, Sheol, Hades, and Gehenna. Often the Bosom of Abraham, Sheol, and Hades were considered the waiting places where righteous Jews would, after death, join with Abraham, Isaac, and Jacob in what some would refer to as paradise. Hades and Gehenna were more often places of torment, the equivalent of what we know as hell.

The theology of what happened to the righteous Jews wasn't fully developed until after Christ's resurrection. Many Christian theologians today teach what many of the early Christian theologians, including St.

Augustine of Hippo, taught: that this Bosom of Abraham, also called the Limbo of the Patriarchs or Hades, as Jesus described, had two compartments. One was for the righteous, and there was comfort there, while the other compartment was for the unworthy and the evildoers. The compartment that held the righteous was emptied out when Jesus rose from the dead.

This thought or teaching was included in the Apostles' Creed: "He suffered under Pontius Pilate, was crucified, died, and was buried. He descended into hell." Many believe the same is also plainly stated in Peter's epistle: "After being made alive, he [Jesus] went and made proclamation to the imprisoned spirits" (1Pet. 3:19).

Once Christ emptied this good compartment after His resurrection, it seemed logical to some that it would be a good place to place those babies and children who died and were not yet baptized. There was no scriptural teaching that babies who died without being baptized needed a special place to go. However, once the doctrine that water baptism wasn't just symbolic but was essential developed, it did create a need for a limbo.

Interestingly, despite the teachings of the nuns and the common belief of many Roman Catholics, the Roman Catholic Church has no official doctrine on the eternal state of babies. The existence of limbo is not an official teaching of the Roman Catholic Church.[30] However, these are opinions the church does not condemn.

One of the more intriguing comments I found while researching early church teachings on purgatory, indulgences, and limbo was a comment by Cardinal Joseph Ratzinger, who was prefect of the Congregation for the Doctrine of the Faith. Up until 1965 this very high office in the Roman Catholic Church also was known as the head of the Universal Inquisition. Cardinal Joseph Ratzinger became Pope Benedict XVI, and the intriguing comment or quote was: "If purgatory didn't exist, we should have to invent it."[31]

CHAPTER NINETEEN

Celibacy

A Personal Choice or Requirement?

Etching of St. Paphnutius, fourth-century bishop, from a
private collection owned by Collection Cos. Photographic
reproduction and original work in the public domain.

The subject of celibacy really never came up at St. Joseph's Catholic School. It was, however, very well known that neither the priests nor the nuns could be married.

In the 1960s even the smaller parishes were fortunate to have more than one priest to say Masses and provide for the well-being of the congregation. We had three priests at St. Joseph's church during most of our time at the Catholic school. The three priests included a semiretired monsignor, who was a character. He was likely in his late sixties or early seventies at the time. As an altar boy, serving with the monsignor was always interesting, as he had the habit of starting Mass when he was ready regardless of whether we were ready or if it was time for Mass or not.

There were many times we boys would be running behind him, trying to snap up our cassocks under our starchy, white surplices. My parents liked it when he said Mass as well, as he would often abbreviate many of the readings and get the people in and out in about thirty minutes.

There seemed to be plenty of nuns at the time. They all lived together in the two-story convent directly behind the school, and all were unmarried. They wore very traditional black and white habits; long, black veils; and long rosaries attached to belts around their waists. While it was not unusual for us to see a priest in different clothing, without a collar or even in shorts, the nuns were rarely ever seen out of their standard habits or with any accessories other than purses. The only things that changed were their shoes and, during the cold winters, the dark wool coats that were popular among the nuns and looked pretty warm.

While there may have been a movement in some circles to allow the priests to marry or to change the rules about celibacy back in the 1960s, it was unknown to us. This was before cable TV, the Internet, and a constant, twenty-four-hour news cycle. The NBC, CBS, and ABC news media and their local affiliates rarely if ever featured any news about the Catholic Church other than sports scores for their seemingly dominant football teams.

Today the issue of celibacy is a popular topic with both the uninformed and the opinionated. In the United States as well as in many nations around the globe, the Catholic Church has had to face very serious issues of child sexual abuse allegations and convictions. Some connect the alleged crimes to the church's practice of celibacy. The thinking is that somehow celibacy creates pent-up sexual frustration that is then released through criminal conduct.

However, while the child sexual abuse allegations are very serious and no child should be subjected to abuse, there is no evidence I have found that priests are more likely to abuse children than are other groups of men. The Center for Sex Offender Management (CSOM) has stated repeatedly that there is no profile of a typical sex offender.[32] If that is true, then child sex offenders can be male or female, married, divorced, or single. Research indicates that the majority of the offenders are minors themselves, typically older boys preying on younger boys and girls. It follows, therefore, that only a very small percentage of these sex offenders would be frustrated because of celibacy.

The news reports of clergy sexual abuse, just like other stories of infidelity, theft, power struggles, or any kind of abuse within the church, have wounded the church and created a blemish on the desirability of a career or vocational calling to the priesthood. Many people believe that celibacy has contributed greatly to the decline in the number of priests. In total the number of Catholic priests in the United States dropped from nearly 59,000 in 1975 to about 41,500 last year.[33]

These issues, coupled with other demographic and macro trends in the Catholic Church, have led to a serious decline in the number of men going into the priesthood.

The requirement of celibate priests in the church is ancient, meaning the advocacy of celibacy for both priests and monks dates back centuries. The picture at the beginning of this chapter is of Origen, who was born at the end of the second century in Alexandria, Egypt. The Alexandrian school was one of the first advocates of monastic living, including a very ascetic lifestyle that was void of all material comforts. Origen was famous for being a devoted Christian, an early theologian, a heretic, and an early advocate for celibacy (not all at the same time). So passionate was he about his own celibacy that he reportedly castrated himself.

The celibacy of the priesthood in the Roman Catholic Church is a discipline, not a doctrine. This means it can be changed, though there doesn't seem to be much movement at the top indicating it will change anytime soon. The definition of celibacy in the Roman Catholic Church is also slightly different in that it strictly refers to the requirement that their priests remain unmarried. This is not at all to indicate that the Roman Catholic Church is not interested in purity or chastity, as there are vows that all priests take regarding the sins of the flesh.

There has been much research into the origins of the celibate priest movement. Most of the apostles were married, Peter was married, and seven popes were married. Likely the teachings of Gnosticism that material things and sexual relations even in marriage were evil led to the teachings on celibacy.

The first recorded requirement of celibacy was issued at the Synod of Elvira (circa AD 305–306). This same synod also issued injunctions against the use of any pictures inside the church "so that they do not become objects of worship and adoration" and that "candles are not to be burned in a cemetery during the day."[34] It was not unusual for many of the councils to have injunctions or proclamations that were later reversed or even considered heresy.

For example, just a few years after Elvira, Constantine called the First Ecumenical Council of the church, with many bishops in attendance from both the East and the West. At this council in AD 325, officially called the Council of Nicaea, there was a discussion on clerical celibacy. The council disagreed with the requirements handed down by the Synod of Elvira. They agreed with the Egyptian bishop—St. Paphnutius, the confessor of Thebes—who argued successfully that celibacy should be only a matter of personal choice and not a requirement.

Church clergy remained married without any restrictions until Pope Pelagious II (AD 579–590) issued a series of proclamations regarding celibacy that were designed primarily to stop property from being transferred from clergy to children. However, this papal proclamation was often ignored.

It was not until the Second Lateran Council in AD 1139 that the Latin (Western) Rite of the Catholic Church decided to accept people for ordination only after they had taken a promise of celibacy.

The Eastern Orthodox Church continues to follow the thinking of St. Paphnutius. To this day about 90 percent of all Orthodox clerics are married.

CHAPTER TWENTY

Communion and the Mass

The Agape Feast

Última Cena (Last Supper) by Leonardo da Vinci (1452–1519). Location: Convent of Santa Maria del Grazie, Milan, Italy. Photographic reproduction and original work in the public domain.

Sister Mary Justina was our second-grade teacher at St. Joseph's Catholic School. As we entered second grade, she reminded both students and parents that we had a serious year with some serious school-work ahead of us.

Catholic schools were known not only for their strict discipline and uniforms but also for some great academic programs. St. Joseph's was no exception, and very quickly in the year we were introduced to our first story problems—a clever way of introducing both math and reading into stories that needed to be fully understood as well as solved. It seemed like Johnny always had his apples taken away and was left with less than he had when he began.

Reading was also a big part the academic emphasis, and one of my favorites was our subscription to *Highlights for Children*. These were not just for Catholics but had great adventure stories, articles about animals, some games, and hidden-word puzzles. They also had poems, some American history, and contemporary issues, one of which was the new Polio vaccine that was being administered to school children across the country.

Spelling was important to the nuns, and even in second grade we were expected to be able to write complete sentences with all words spelled correctly. Every week we had new spelling lists, and spelling bees were a typical Friday afternoon activity.

I was never very good at spelling, and I'm delighted that spell check has been a feature on computers and laptops for a few decades now. I never figured out why spelling bees rewarded those who spelled the words incorrectly by allowing us to go back to our desks and sit down. I was typically sitting by the second or third round.

Sister Mary Justina also had the responsibility of getting her second-grade class ready for our first Communion. There were about forty of us in the class. Today that would be an excessive student-to-teacher ratio, but Sister Mary Justina had no problems keeping us in line and all attentive to whatever she was trying to teach.

Preparation for first Communion took the entire year, as it was typically held in the spring. There were prayers we needed to memorize.

These included the Our Father, the Hail Mary, and the Glory Be. Our teacher also introduced us to the Ten Commandments, though they were shortened to help us memorize them more easily: we committed "no other gods, no swearing, keep the Sabbath, honor your parents" to memory, and eventually we could recite them all by heart.

Along with the preparation for first Communion, we had to make our first Confession, which was a little scarier than Communion, as we had to go into a dark confessional and be able to recite the official Act of Contrition. At the time our sins were not very serious, though we all knew that Alan Hebert, the class bully, probably had a lot to confess.

When Communion day finally arrived, the girls all wore beautiful white dresses. The boys just wore new sport coats and slacks, and all of us had the same blue bow ties and white armbands. I never did figure out the significance of the boys' attire. The girls, of course, immediately associated their attire with wedding dresses, which was probably the intention all along.

Most Roman Catholics—and, for the most part, most Christians—don't think too much about the history of some of their traditions. Growing up Catholic, we also assumed and usually were taught that the sacraments, customs, and traditions we followed had always been and likely would always be.

Of course everything seemed to change in 1965, when the Second Vatican Council made some major changes to the Mass, changing the language from Latin to English here in the United States.

All of my research has revealed that there have been many changes over the years in the sacraments in the church, and that includes the Roman Catholic sacrament of the Eucharist.

Most of us are aware that all Christian Communion practices have their beginnings in the Last Supper of Jesus and His apostles. That Last Supper was actually a Seder meal, and many contemporary Jews would recognize many of the elements—the sharing of the cup, the blessing, the breaking of bread, the sop that was handed to Judas—as part of their Passover celebrations.

The New Testament's book of Acts 2:42 records that early Christians would gather together to worship, pray, and teach. In the years after the church was empowered by the Holy Spirit at Pentecost, there were two different but similar customs or early sacraments that are closely related to the more contemporary practice of Communion. These two sacraments could also be called meals, as one was the Lord's Supper and the other was the Agape feast.

In 1 Corinthians 11:20–22, the apostle Paul was critical of the church because they were getting too rowdy and even drunk at what others would later call the Agape love feast:

> Therefore, when you come together, it is not really to eat the Lord's Supper. For at the meal, each one eats his own supper ahead of others. So one person is hungry while another gets drunk! Don't you have houses to eat and drink in? Or do you look down on the church of God and embarrass those who have nothing? What should I say to you? Should I praise you? I do not praise you for this! (HCSB)

Many scholars believe the early church would gather weekly for a common meal, often shared in the homes or house churches. Each meal would include a blessing, the breaking of bread, and a distribution of Communion. Over time this Communion (a Greek word for "fellowship") became the Eucharist (another Greek word, meaning "grateful" or "thanksgiving") and the central focus of the weekly gathering.

Piecing various historical records together indicates that this weekly common meal, sometimes called the Agape feast, included the distribution of Communion. However, independent of the Agape feast, a separate liturgy developed for Communion that did not include a meal.

The Agape feast was truly a feast (think potluck with wine), and, probably because of the abuses similar to those mentioned by Paul hundreds of years earlier, it disappeared completely by the fourth century. The apostle Jude also mentioned these Agape (meaning "love") feasts and some problematic individuals. He wrote that some people were "spots in your love feasts, while they feast with you without fear, serving only themselves" (Jude 1:12, NKJV).

Weekly celebrations, services, and the beginnings of what Roman Catholics now know as the Mass were anything but uniform throughout the early church. Cultural differences, location, language, and distance all had impacts on the way these early Christians would relate to each other, gather, and worship.

History records that the head of some of the local churches were called presidents, though in some locations, and over time, the heads of the church were referred to by the Greek words *presbuteros* and *episkopos*, typically translated as "elders" and "bishops." Typically the duty of breaking bread and distributing Communion was the duty of these leaders of the church.

Both history and the Bible give us indications that the early Christian community would utilize primarily Jewish prayers of thanksgiving on the Sabbath in connection with the breaking of bread and the distribution of Communion, which was their Last Supper memorial. As the believers in Jesus were removed from the Jewish houses of worship, they began to meet officially on Sundays, which was called the Lord's Day. The apostle John, writing in Revelation 1:10, said, "On the Lord's Day I was in the Spirit, and I heard behind me a loud voice like a trumpet."

By the end of the first century, Christians began to identify their weekly gatherings as pure sacrifice as opposed to the public sacrifices to the gods, which they referred to as offerings to demons. As the apostolic community was no longer on the scene, the church would use, read, and reflect on the writings of the first-generation leaders, including the writings of Paul and the sacred writings that would become the New Testament. Various patterned prayers, singing, invocations, and remembrances were added that ultimately developed into the beginnings of what is recognized by the Roman Catholic Church as the liturgy of the word.

The concept of the bread and wine being the body and blood of Jesus was acknowledged sufficiently in the second and third centuries that the Romans accused the Christians of being cannibals. There has been much controversy in the church surrounding the actual presence of Christ in the memorial service that we know as the Eucharist or Communion. We will not try to settle this controversy, but we can look at some history and some practical comments related to the development of the doctrine.

History records that over time, theologians identified the Eucharist as both a memorial ritual as well as a sacrificial ritual. The Eucharist was said to be both the reenactment of the Last Supper along with a strong identification of the bread and wine with the body and blood of Jesus.

The question that arises is whether the bread and wine were symbolic and a memorial or whether there was a sacrifice and a transubstantiation—the Catholic Church term indicating the bread and wine become literally the body and blood of Jesus.

By the fourth century, some of the modern teachings of the Roman Catholic Church had evolved, but not with the clarity that many would suppose. For example, we have writings by both St. Augustine (bishop in Hippo, Africa) as well as Cyril (archbishop of Jerusalem) related to the Eucharist. Augustine said Jesus is present in the Eucharist "*per modum symboli*," or symbolically.[35] However, Cyril declared that in the Eucharist, Christians "offer up Christ sacrificed for our sins."[36] Obviously there was nothing symbolic about the way Cyril viewed the Eucharist.

From my perspective the issue is not about the presence of Christ but the ability of a man, a Roman Catholic priest, to be able to transform supernaturally, call down, or have the power to change bread and wine into the actual body and blood of Christ. This is a role or a power that other ordained clergy or pastors of various other churches do not claim to have or believe is appropriate.

The issue of symbolic versus actual is an argument that may not need to be voiced. Symbols are often actual representations. For example, the national seal of a country on an embassy in a foreign land indicates not symbolically but in actuality that the embassy is a part of that nation, even though it may be thousands of miles from the homeland. The American flag is not a mere symbol but represents the country. That is why patriots will come to the rescue of the flag that is burning or being dishonored in some way. Are a married couple's wedding rings merely symbols? If they were, why would they be one of the central elements in a wedding ceremony and thought to be literally priceless if lost or stolen? Misplace your wedding ring someday, and see if your spouse thinks it was just symbolic.

Both the traditions as well as the teachings of the church changed considerably over the first few centuries. By the fourth century, the first Christian emperor, Constantine, eliminated the persecution of the Christians, which led to the rapid expansion of Christianity in the empire. Around that time the local pastors of the church were first being called priests, a term that would never have been used for the leaders of the church at the time of the apostles. Priests were nonexistent in the church for the first few hundred years, but *priest* became the popular term for the clergy that were ordained and commissioned. As the priests took on this specialized role, the laity took an increasingly diminished role in spiritual affairs.

Soon the clergy started dressing differently from the rest of the church, and Latin became the official language of the church. Soon those who didn't speak Latin (including nearly all of Europe after the fall of Rome in the fifth century) couldn't read the Bible or understand the prayers and liturgy of the Mass.

There was a great amount of diversity in traditions and practices in the church. However, by the seventh century, Pope Gregory declared that the Latin Mass used in Rome was the standard, and it became the basis for what Roman Catholics knew as the Roman rite up until the time of the Second Vatican Council in the 1960s.

In the Middle Ages, the sacraments were fully defined, the power of the church became absolute, and the sacrificial aspect of the Eucharist grew in importance while the Last Supper and meal symbolism diminished. The spiritual divide between the clergy and laity widened. The power of the priesthood was thought to be essential in the celebration and the sacrifice of the Mass. For the most part, the general public became merely spectators to an intentionally mysterious drama that the priest performed while wearing special robes and standing before an altar.

The Eucharistic prayers, consecration, and Communion became the central part of the worship service. However, the people rarely participated, as they were reminded frequently of their sins and shortcomings. The importance of receiving Communion became less important for the laity than their witness at the Mass of the consecration of the bread and wine. This led to the practice of worshipping and adoring the Eucharistic Lord (the specialized round wafer, called a host, from the Latin *hostia*, meaning "an offering, usually an animal").

Because so few people were receiving Holy Communion, the Fourth Lateran Council (AD 1215) required that Catholics must receive Communion at least once a year.

The sixteenth century brought about the Protestant Reformation. The pope convened the Council of Trent (1545–1563) to correct some of the abuses that had crept into the church. It also defended some Catholic beliefs that the reformers attacked. In the area of the Eucharist, the church fathers reaffirmed the real presence of Jesus. They also defended the sacrificial nature of the Mass against the reformers. In addition the Roman Missal was published, which brought uniformity to the official ritual of the Mass. The Roman Catholic Church used it for the next four hundred years.

Most Catholics continued to avoid going to Communion, believing they were unworthy, until 1910, when Pope Pius X permitted children who attained the age of reason to receive Holy Communion and encouraged frequent Communion by all the faithful.

More than anything else, it was Pius X's reforms of the Eucharist that had the greatest impact on the daily lives of Catholics. With his decree, *"Sacra Tridentina Synodus"* (1905), Pius emphasized that Holy Communion was not a reward for good behavior but, as the Council of Trent noted, "the antidote whereby we may be freed from daily faults and be preserved from mortal sins." In another decree, *"Quam Singulari"* (1910), the pope laid out guidelines on the age of children who are to be admitted to Holy Communion. In the past, children—or better, adolescents—received their first Communions when they were between the ages of twelve and fourteen. Since Pius X's edict, they were more likely around seven years of age, often in the second grade, as I was at St. Joseph's School.

CHAPTER TWENTY-ONE

Transubstantiation

This Is My Body

Last Supper by Giotto (1266–1337). Fresco from 1304, from a chapel in Padua, Italy. Photographic reproduction and original work in the public domain.

There is probably no greater difference of opinion among theologians than in the Roman Catholic doctrine of transubstantiation.

There are various theological definitions of the Eucharist and the presence or symbolic representation of Christ in the sacrament. Many have tried to use Greek or Latin-derived multisyllable words to describe it, but in the end it remains a mystery. One of the most appropriate quotes I found regarding the presence of Christ in the Eucharist is from John of Damascus (AD 665–749), a Syrian monk and priest. Born and raised in Damascus, he said:

> And now you ask how the bread becomes the body of Christ, and the wine and the water become the blood of Christ. I shall tell you. The Holy Spirit comes upon them, and achieves things which surpass every word and thought. Let it be enough for you to understand that this takes place by the Holy Spirit.[37]

This simple explanation has not been sufficient for most theologians. Over the years, and particularly since the Protestant Reformation, countless volumes have been written regarding the nuances of the Eucharist, with strong opinions on the various viewpoints. These are not simple "either-or" choices but a cornucopia of overly complicated and confusing doctrines that are both exhaustive and exhausting.

My approach will be different. Since this book attempts to reconcile rather than divide, I'll suggest some simple, distinctive understandings of the Eucharist, particularly with regard to this concept of the real presence of Christ as well as the Roman Catholic doctrine of transubstantiation.

At the heart of this subject are three separate but closely related topics or doctrines that have been developed over the years. These are the three distinctive differences that unnecessarily separate the Body of Christ. However, my objective is to understand that all can be seen as examples of the diversity within the Body of Christ that the church has experienced not only over time, but also at the same time.

For example, if the first-century church didn't believe something exactly the way the church later came to believe, are not both the first-century church and the latter church both still the church? If so, then the diversity of doctrines that are embraced today by individuals who continue to believe the essential faith and adhere to the clear Gospel of Jesus Christ are examples of the diversity within one church and not a divided church.

I have done the research and can state that I can defend all these examples of diversity within the same Body of Christ with logic, history, and scripture. Some theologians will disagree, but they have already written their books. It's now my turn.

The three distinctive doctrines, or teachings, are as follows, and each will be developed separately:

1) The presence of Christ in the Eucharist or Communion.
2) The agency of the priest in the sacrament of the Eucharist.
3) The sacrificial aspect of the sacrament.

The presence of Christ in the Eucharist or Communion

As I mentioned in the previous chapter, the concept of the bread and wine being the body and blood of Jesus was acknowledged sufficiently in the second and third centuries that the Romans accused the Christians of being cannibals. From the very beginning of the church, Christian gatherings often included the commemoration of the Lord's Supper. Over time this became the sacrament of the Eucharist, or what many refer to as Communion.

While there are a great variety of doctrines regarding how real the presence of Christ is in the sacrament, most theologians would agree that the early church took the words of Jesus referring to His body and His blood very seriously, if not literally. The best quote I can use regarding Christ's presence in the sacrament is from the Bible: "The cup of blessing that we give thanks for, is it not a sharing in the blood of Christ?

The bread that we break, is it not a sharing in the body of Christ?" (1 Cor. 10:16, HCSB).

St. Augustine wrote about Communion in the fourth century. He said Jesus was present in the Eucharist *"per modum symboli."*[38] This belief in the presence of Christ in the sacrament of Communion, however, is not the doctrine of transubstantiation. That Roman Catholic doctrine was not clearly defined until after the Reformation. The word *transubstantiation* was used to refer to the mysterious change that many believed occurred at some point during the ceremony. The word was first used by Thomas Aquinas, a Dominican Priest (OP), philosopher, and theologian of the thirteenth century who adopted a concept regarding matter and substance that was developed by the Greek philosopher Aristotle.

The word itself has everything to do with the change and not the presence. The word derives from Latin—*trans* ("across") and *substantia* ("substance")—and indicates that the bread is transformed into the actual flesh of Christ and the wine or grape juice into the actual blood of Christ. Many Christians throughout the centuries have fully believed Jesus was present in the Eucharist or Communion but may not have embraced this very specific and later-developed doctrine.

Christ's presence in the Eucharist or Communion through the ages and in various churches is characterized somewhat differently. For example, is Christ present in the actual bread and wine, or is He present with the community and those who partake of the sacrament? These are just two seemingly differing views, but theologians can take these two and create hundreds of different variations.

Jesus's first and only celebration of the Lord's Supper was on the night before He died. When He said, "This is my body" and "This is my blood," He was referring to the bread and the wine; at the same time He was fully present and reclining with the apostles. In talking about the real presence of Christ in the Sacrament, theologians also try to address which body of Christ is present, as the Bible tells us the resurrected body of Jesus is not exactly the same body He had at the time of the Last Supper.

For many people the real presence of Christ does not necessarily need to be a physical presence in the bread and wine, nor does it mean that it is some spiritual phantasm or ghostly presence. The Holy Spirit was really present at Pentecost and was physically manifest in tongues like fire (Acts 2:3). However, the Holy Spirit also is really present in the life of every spirit-filled believer in Jesus Christ.

> And if the Spirit of him who raised Jesus from the dead
> lives in you, then He who raised Christ from the dead will
> also bring your mortal bodies to life through His Spirit
> who lives in you. (Rom. 8:11, HCSB)

Many theologians seem to enjoy arguing about the nuances of the actual presence of Christ in the sacrament. Roman Catholics and Eastern Orthodox are most closely aligned, but they disagree on how this mystery is accomplished. I find it interesting to note that the Vatican typically uses the word *mystery* when referring to these beliefs, including the Eucharist and the Mass, but then the theologians attempt to explain the mystery when, by definition, a mystery is something that cannot be explained!

While the Roman Catholic Church officially embraces transubstantiation, the Orthodox (Greek, Coptic, Russian, Antioch, Eastern, etc.) holds to a doctrine called consubstantiation. However, both branches (East and West) of the Catholic Church embrace the belief that Christ is literally and physically present in the Communion elements.

While Protestantism is thought sometimes to have a different viewpoint, there has been an evolution of belief in Protestantism and a great deal of variety in teachings regarding the sacrament of the Eucharist or Communion and the presence of Christ.

Martin Luther is said to have started the Protestant Reformation in 1515, though there were many previous reformers and even revivals that can be dated to hundreds of years earlier. Lutherans today have developed various teachings regarding the real presence of Christ in the sacrament; however, most still utilize the Augsburg Confession of 1530 as one of their foundational confessions or beliefs. This is a number of confessions expressed in twenty-eight articles that set forth what Lutherans are to believe. Augsburg Confession Article 10 states, "About the Supper of the Lord they teach that the Body and Blood of Christ are truly present, and are distributed."

Some churches, such as those that have Methodist and Wesleyan roots, would agree that Jesus is fully present in Communion, just as He is present in the reading of the word of God. This is a clear departure from a physical presence but still embraced as a mystery, though it lacks the specificity of the doctrines of the Roman Catholics or Orthodox.

John Calvin was one of the great theologians of the Reformation, and his teachings have influenced all of the Reformed Churches (i.e., Presbyterian, Reformed, Christian Reformed) and Calvinist Churches. His teaching on the sacrament of the Eucharist was explained more in the terms of the believer's mystical union with Christ. He explained in his *Institutes of the Christian Religion* (1536) that just as baptism is connected with the believer's initiation into union with Christ, the Lord's Supper strengthens the believer's ongoing union with Christ.

Today many Evangelicals have embraced a teaching that Communion is primarily symbolic and a memorial. According to a 1994 *New York Times* study,[39] half of the Catholics who attended Mass regularly believed similarly that the bread and the wine symbolically represented the presence of Christ.

Communion for many Evangelicals (rarely would an Evangelical use the word *Eucharist*) is a very special ordinance or sacrament of the church. It has been my observation that there seems to be a growing number of Evangelical Churches that are celebrating Communion more frequently, with more solemnity and much greater reverence.

The Agency of the Priest in the Sacrament of the Eucharist

The Reformation of the sixteenth century was a major turning point for the church. In many ways it marked the beginning of the end of the all-too-often cozy relationship between the church and the state. At the heart of the Reformation was the belief that it was the Bible and not centuries of tradition that should be the primary rule or guide for matters of faith.

Many have heard the terms *sola scriptura* ("scripture alone") and *sola fide* ("faith alone") in regard to the teachings that emerged during the Reformation. Just as important was a third theological issue, which was the priesthood of all believers.

This teaching had two major consequences. First, it elevated the state of the laity from casual observers, subjects, and second-class citizens of the church to the belief taken from 1 Peter 2:15 that all believers are priests before God. This means that believers would have direct access to God through Jesus Christ and would be responsible for their own faith, beliefs, and actions.

The second and possibly greater consequence of the theological teaching of the priesthood of all believers was the initial rejection of the pope as the vicar of Christ and ultimately the rejection of the Catholic priests as necessary mediators of the sacraments and agents of God to bring grace. Grace in the teachings of the reformers was defined to be the unmerited favor of God, and people could not earn grace through the actions of a priest.

The ramifications of this teaching brought about a thoroughly exhaustive reexamination of the teaching of the Roman Catholic Church on the sacrament of the Eucharist, the agency of the priest in the sacrament, and the doctrine of transubstantiation.

The Roman Catholic Church didn't call a council to address the Reformation, started on October 31, 1517, by Martin Luther and lasting until 1545. By that time hope for reconciliation between various Christian Churches and teachings were slim. Many of the Reformation Churches looked and behaved in many ways like the Roman Catholic Churches and in fact were in the same locations and often led by many of the same people. Other Protestant Churches, however, were drastically different from their Roman Catholic brethren, and as Protestant leaders gained power, they too often showed they could be as intolerant of people who disagreed with their doctrine as the pope and the Church of Rome.

The Council of Trent reaffirmed the Roman Catholic teaching of transubstantiation and very clearly rejected the Protestant teaching. The biggest issue in the Eucharist was exactly the agency, or the power, of the Roman Catholic priest to transform the elements into the actual body and blood of Jesus Christ. The Council of Trent affirmed it; the Protestants for the most part completely rejected it. By the time of the Council of Trent, the doctrines of *sola scriptura, sola fide,* and the priesthood of all believers made the agency of an official Roman Catholic priest in the sacrament of the Eucharist for nearly half of the world's Christians unnecessary; in fact it was often seen as contrary to the teachings in the Bible.

The Sacrificial Aspect of the Sacrament

In Roman Catholic tradition, the sacrificial nature of the Mass and its central element, the Eucharist, is paramount. This is one of the reasons why the liturgy of the Catholic Mass is so different in so many aspects from the liturgies of both non-Catholic Churches and nonliturgical churches as well.

While we demonstrated that the real presence of Christ in the sacrament of the Eucharist or Communion was not an either-or but a wide continuum of beliefs and practices, it is not true for the sacrificial nature of the sacrament.

The earliest known reference to the Eucharist being a sacrifice is found in the Didache, or the Teaching of the Twelve Apostles. This document was discovered in a monastery in 1883 and is in all likelihood one of the most disputed early Christian texts. It does, however, shed some light on very ancient teachings within the church and has a part that is often quoted by proponents of the Eucharist as a sacrifice:

> On the Lord's own day, assemble in common to break bread and offer thanks. But first confess your sins so that your sacrifice may be pure. However, no one quarreling with his brother may join your meeting until they are

reconciled; your sacrifice must not be defiled. (Teaching of the Twelve Apostles, 14.1)

While the authenticity of the document can be debated, it can also be noted that while the word *sacrifice* is mentioned, it isn't clear that it is referring to the specific doctrine related to the Eucharist that developed over the centuries.

It is true that we have a number of references and historical writings from the second and third centuries that clearly refer to the Eucharist as a sacrifice. The issue that remains, however, is: When did the church begin to teach that the Mass itself was a reenactment of the actual crucifixion of the Lord?

By AD 350 Cyril (AD 313–AD 386), the archbishop of Jerusalem, discussed the Eucharist prayer. In his writings he said that Christians "offer up Christ, sacrificed for our sins."[40]

The Lord's Supper is recounted by the apostle Paul in his first letter to the Corinthians:

> For I received from the Lord what I also passed on to you: On the night when he was betrayed, the Lord Jesus took bread, gave thanks, broke it, and said, "This is My body, which is for you. Do this in remembrance of Me." In the same way, after supper He also took the cup and said, "This cup is the new covenant established by My blood. Do this, as often as you drink it, in remembrance of Me." For as often as you eat this bread and drink the cup, you proclaim the Lord's death until He comes. (1 Cor. 11: 23–26)

These words are part of the Roman Catholic Liturgy, and they occur during the most sacred part of the Mass: the consecration. While the Protestant Reformers rejected the agency of the Roman Catholic priest in the Eucharist or Communion, the Council of Trent confirmed the earlier teaching of the Roman Catholic Church that it was at the Last

Supper that Jesus instituted not a memorial nor a meal, but a visible sacrifice, following in the very same way the Levitical priesthood.

In chapter 1 of the "Doctrines on the Sacrifice of the Mass," the council wrote:

> That He might leave, to His own beloved Spouse the church, a visible sacrifice, such as the nature of man requires, whereby that bloody sacrifice, once to be accomplished on the cross, might be represented, and the memory thereof remain even unto the end of the world...He offered up to God the Father His own body and blood under the species of bread and wine; and, under the symbols of those same things, He delivered (His own body and blood) to be received by His apostles, whom He then constituted priests of the New Testament; and by those words, Do this in commemoration of me, He commanded them and their successors in the priesthood, to offer (them); even as the Catholic Church has always understood and taught.[41]

Nearly the entire liturgy of the Mass is designed intentionally to reinforce this mysterious reenactment of the sacrifice of Jesus on the cross. According to the Roman Catholic Church, the Mass is the sacrifice of the new law in which Christ, through the ministry of the priest, offers Himself to God in an unbloody manner under the appearances of bread and wine.[42]

Other aspects of the Mass also reinforce this teaching of its sacrificial nature. There is the specialized round wafer, called a host, from the Latin *hostia*, meaning, as noted earlier, "a sacrificial offering, usually an animal." In addition the word *priest* is important in this discussion. This was not a term used for the clergy in the apostolic era or into the first century. The early officers of the church were elders and deacons. The local head of a congregation was called a president. The word *priest* is not the English translation of the word *presbyter* or *elder* but is a translation of the Greek word *hierus,* found often in the Bible and always translated as the word *priest.*

The word *hierus* is found in the Greek New Testament thirty-one times and is always in reference to the Jewish priests or pagan priests, with the exception of Hebrews 5–7, in which case the writer compared Jesus to the true high priest. Then, in the book of Revelation, we are called a nation of kings and priests. In 1 Peter 2:9 we are called a chosen race, a royal priesthood (Greek: *hierateuma*).

In their disagreement with Rome, the reformers rejected the sacrificial nature of the Mass. One of the key verses they used was a very large section out of the book of Hebrews, chapter 10. I am copying the entire passage for two reasons. The first is that it is good to see what the verse is referring to in context. The second reason is that these verses spoke very clearly to me in my early walk with Christ:

> Every priest stands day after day ministering and offering the same sacrifices time after time, which can never take away sins. But this man, after offering one sacrifice for sins forever, sat down at the right hand of God. He is now waiting until His enemies are made His footstool. For by one offering He has perfected forever those who are sanctified. The Holy Spirit also testifies to us about this. For after He says:
>
> This is the covenant I will make with them after those days, says the Lord: I will put My laws on their hearts and write them on their minds,
>
> He adds:
> I will never again remember their sins and their lawless acts.
>
> Now where there is forgiveness of these, there is no longer an offering for sin. (Heb. 10:11–18)

CHAPTER TWENTY-TWO

Latin

In Nòmine Patris

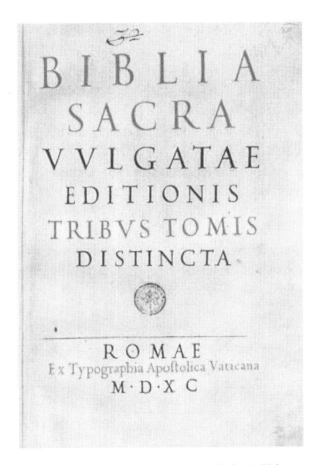

The above image is the cover page of the Latin Vulgate
bible, authorized in Rome in the fourth century and
printed in 1590. Photographic reproduction and original
work in the public domain.

Some may be asking: why a chapter on Latin? Well, for those who are old enough to remember the days before the Second Vatican Council, Latin was the language of the Mass. Prior to the Protestant Reformation, it was the only language of the Bible and the church.

At St. Joseph's Catholic School, not every boy entering fourth grade became an altar boy, but most of my friends wanted to, and I thought it was a great way to get some special privileges. And it just seemed like a cool thing to do.

With my parents' permission, I started lessons on becoming an altar boy along with eleven other boys. We met after our last class on Tuesdays for about two hours, and on the first day we received a book—*Learning to Serve: A Guide for New Altar Boys.*[43]

Only boys were allowed to serve at the time; girls wouldn't have that privilege for another twenty years. The *Learning to Serve* books contained twenty-five short chapters. Many if not all of them were about the honor and privilege of serving as an altar boy. Some chapters, however, also included listings and definitions of the Latin words we needed to know. Some of the words were for objects and things that were ceremonially used, and we learned the official names of the parts of the Mass. Some were old Latin words that had made their way into the English language, including *cruets*, which were the small glass crystal vessels for the wine and the water that were used in the Mass.

I paged through the book and was relieved I really didn't need to learn Latin, just a few words. Since the entire Mass was said in Latin, Catholics were familiar with some of the Latin responses and prayers. The most common responses were *"amen,"* which means exactly the same thing in Latin as it does in English; *"Kyrie eleison,"* or "Lord have mercy"; and *"Christe eleison,"* or "Christ have mercy."

When I was in my prime as an altar boy, the Second Vatican Council issued a new sacred liturgy, and most Catholic parishes in the United States and Canada implemented it in early 1965. For English-speaking Catholics, the change was radical. For the first time the priest would say the Mass from the initial greetings through the liturgy of the Word, the liturgy of the Eucharist, and the concluding rites all in English.

Catholics seemed generally positive about the change, but a very vocal minority wanted the old ways and the Latin Mass to stay.

While the Latin Mass had been around for centuries, it wasn't the language of the apostles or of the scriptures. Scholars all agree that Jesus spoke Aramaic and Hebrew and probably was familiar with Greek. The New Testament was written likely in Greek, and ancient fragments of very early copies of some of the epistles of Paul and the Gospels are also in Greek.

So when did Latin become the language of the church? Why did the church translate the Bible into Latin? The answer to that question is much more than just a date in history, as it also became a watershed moment in the church and would become one of the single most important cultural aspects in the church in the West for more than thirteen hundred years.

The Greek language at the time of Christ and for the next few hundred years was the universal language in Europe. While local dialects and languages were always the mother tongue, Greek was used in a similar way that many educated people in the world use English today. The Greeks had conquered much of Europe and the Middle East, but while the Roman Empire replaced and surpassed them, Koine Greek continued to be not only the language of business and commerce but was encouraged among the learned and the scholars.

By the fourth century AD, however, things had changed. Latin, the language of Rome, was becoming more common as the language of business and commerce as well as the language of the scholars. The great doctor of the church and the scholar St. Augustine (AD 354–430), for example, wrote extensively in Latin. He was born in North Africa and educated in Rome.

The scriptures, both the Old Testament and the New Testament, by this time had been combined into one collection we know as the Bible. The best translations were still in Greek, though the growing popularity of Latin required the commissioning of an acceptable translation in Latin.

St. Jerome was born in modern-day Bosnia around the year AD 342 and traveled to Rome around AD 360. There he was baptized and began his higher education and studies into the church and languages, including Hebrew, Greek, and Latin. While the best Bible translations were in Greek, there was also a very accurate and scholarly version in Syriac, an ancient language similar to Aramaic and Hebrew. At the time of Jerome's education in Rome, the Latin translations of the Bible were considered substandard, as the Latin Old Testament had been translated from the Greek rather than the original Hebrew. A translation of a translation is never as good as an original translation.

Jerome was quite the scholar, and the bishop of Rome, Damasus the First (known by the Roman Catholic Church as Pope Damasus), appointed him to be his researcher and secretary. According to church records, Damasus I commissioned Jerome to make an acceptable and standard Latin translation of the Bible that would be used by all the people. The result of Jerome's amazing work was the Latin Vulgate, which he completed in AD 400.

What is most interesting about the Latin Vulgate is that even by today's standards, it is a remarkably accurate and faithful translation. Jerome took great care in researching ancient manuscripts in Hebrew and Greek and corrected many of the earlier mistranslations in the Latin texts.

The word *vulgate* comes from the same Latin root word that gives us the English word *vulgar*. This is not at all to imply the "evil, offensive, or rude" meanings of the word, but instead the less common usage meaning "base, common, or ordinary."

Language continually evolves, and within a few hundred years Latin was no longer the common language. This is actually the most disappointing and ironic development in Jerome's work. What had been intended as a translation of the Bible in the common language of the people soon became the official and only acceptable translation in a language that the common people could not read. While Greek had remained the language of the people and the Church in the East, in the West all liturgies were written in Latin, and the Bible was permitted only in Latin. While Latin remained the ecclesiastical, or church, language in the Western (i.e., Roman Catholic) Church, the language of the people eventually developed into separate languages, including Spanish, Portuguese, French, Italian, and Romanian. These languages are known as the Romance languages, and all are derived from Latin.

The Church's insistence on Latin was in part a desire to have "one holy catholic and apostolic church."[44] All too often church unity was thought of in terms of conformity, meaning the same liturgies, same prayers, same Bible, same leadership, and same language. As the church became powerful and fully aligned with the government, the desire for conformity often led to persecution of those who disagreed with various aspects of church doctrine, teaching, or culture. I believe this issue of language was one of the major reasons for the Great Schism of AD 1054, which I will discuss in the next chapter. It permanently separated the Eastern Greek-speaking church from the Western Latin-speaking church.

The Renaissance and Gutenberg's development of the printing press in 1445 created a resurgence in education and a desire for the written word of God. Most attempts to translate the Bible into any language other than Latin, however, were met with great resistance and persecution. John Wyclif, an English scholar and theologian, was an advocate for the Bible and opposed many of the traditions and teachings of the church. He translated the Bible into English in AD 1382 (the Wyclif Bible), and while he escaped martyrdom likely because of the popularity of his followers, called the Lollards, the church declared him a heretic in AD 1415, about thirty years after his death. His bones were exhumed and burned along with his English texts and Bible.

About 150 years after Wyclif, the church again solidified its teachings about the sacred scriptures, and only the clergy were considered worthy to read the Bible. While it was true that few other than the priests could read and understand Latin, Martin Luther charged that too many of the priests were uneducated and unable to but mumble Latin phrases.[45]

William Tyndale (1494–1536) was an English scholar and one of the first to utilize Gutenberg's invention of the printing press to make a translation of the Bible available to English-speaking people. His Bible as well as his theology were considered heretical, and he was arrested, tried, and convicted at a trial in Belgium. On October 6, 1536, he was taken to a prison yard, strangled, and then burned at the stake. His last words were, "Lord, open the king of England's eyes."[46] Scholars note that his prayer was answered. Only a few years later, King Henry VIII authorized the publication of the Great Bible. A few years later, King James would authorize the Bible that to this day includes his name—the King James Version.

The Roman Catholic Church is often criticized for not encouraging the reading of the Bible. From an official standpoint, this is incorrect and a misconception, as historical documents as well as the present catechism of the Catholic Church promote reading of the scriptures:

> The church forcefully and specifically exhorts all the Christian faithful...to learn the surpassing knowledge of Jesus Christ, by frequent reading of the divine Scriptures. Ignorance of the Scriptures is ignorance of Christ. (CCC, 133)

Most historians, however, would point to the time before the Reformation as a season where the laity was unable to read the Latin Vulgate and the Bible was not typically available in other languages. After the Reformation the Protestant emphasis on *sola scriptura* as opposed to church tradition made the Roman Catholic Church clergy suspicious of those who emphasized personal study of the word of God. The Roman Catholic Church since Vatican II has appeared very willing to encourage the laity not only to study and learn the Word of God but to teach and preach and fill roles (such as deacon) that had typically been occupied only by clergy.

CHAPTER TWENTY-THREE

The East-West Schism

The Great Schism of AD 1054

Hagia Sophia Cathedral, Istanbul, Turkey. Built by
Emperor Justinian in the sixth century AD. Photographic
reproduction in the public domain.

"History changes history" was the often-used quote of my favorite high school history teacher, Mr. Everhart. He taught that elections, battles, and events, even those thought to be minor, can and often do have lasting historical impact. Probably nothing is a better example than the rift—or, better described, split—between the Eastern and Western Christian Churches that officially is referred to as the Great Schism of 1054.

It's not unusual that some may get a little confused by the terminology. It was in the early Middle Ages that the word *Catholic* was first used as a reference to the name of the church. The Council of Nicaea used the Greek word *katholikos*, meaning "universal," in reference to the belief in the "one holy, catholic, and apostolic church,"[47] and a few years later, in AD 380, the Roman emperor Theodosius made it official that the name of the church would be *Catholic*. While Emperor Theodosius for a time ruled both the Eastern and Western portions of the Roman Empire, by the fifth century the Western empire had collapsed; Rome had been sacked and no longer had any regional civic influence.

However, in the East, Constantinople continued to be both the head of the Eastern Roman Empire until the fifteenth century and the home of the patriarch, or bishop, of Constantinople. This patriarch exercised considerable influence in the Eastern or Greek-speaking Churches. These Eastern Churches are often called Orthodox or Oriental and officially are known as the Orthodox Catholic Church.

In 1049 a German aristocrat was appointed as successor to Pope Damasus II and took the name Pope Leo IX. Today he is considered one of the most significant popes and a saint in the Roman Catholic Church. In the centuries that had passed since the Council of Nicaea, the Orthodox Church in the East and the Catholic Church in the West had developed different viewpoints on some minor theological issues and one significant leadership issue. The bishop of Rome ruled the Catholic Church of the West almost exclusively and had embraced the name *pope* by the time of Leo the Great in the fifth century.

The Orthodox Church of the East was different and had always embraced the leadership they believed was established and agreed upon at the time of the Council of Nicaea. They were very comfortable in a pentarchy, meaning five patriarchs, or head bishops, would rule over the five geographical areas of the Roman Empire. These patriarchs were located in the important cities of Alexandria, Antioch, Jerusalem, Constantinople, and Rome. While the bishop of Rome was considered first among equals, Orthodox scholars often took the lead in theological areas. They considered Constantinople to be the new Rome and the patriarch of Constantinople to have an unbroken line of apostolic succession and inheritance greater than Rome. They referred to their rich traditions and ceremonies as original and primitive, meaning genuine.

The cultures of the East and West were different as well. In the East, for example, the minor differences in beliefs, ceremonies, leadership, languages, and rites were considered acceptable diversity within the same church. In the West the Catholic bishops and the pope were much more interested in conformity and saw diversity in worship, rites, and leadership as schismatic. They aggressively embraced a unified and ecclesiastical (i.e., church) language, which was Latin, and a church hierarchy that owed complete allegiance to the Pope.

From the fourth to the seventh century, Constantinople was the richest and most powerful center of government in Europe, Africa, or Asia while Western Europe in general and Rome in particular were politically unstable and susceptible to barbarian and foreign attacks. By AD 1049, however, when Pope Leo IX came to power, the Islamic conquests of North Africa, all of the Middle East, ancient Persia, and Armenia had eroded the power of the Orthodox patriarchs in these metropolitan and biblically historical cities. Constantinople ruled from the far eastern edge of an empire that reached to Rome's back door, as the Byzantine Empire included areas adjacent to the papal states, Naples, and Southern Italy, which the Byzantines had taken back from the Islamic invaders.

Whether close proximity brought the ultimate conflict or whether centuries of theological and doctrinal disagreements culminated in the official separation, historians and theologians can argue. The three most likely reasons for the split between Eastern and Western Christianity are the primacy of the bishop of Rome (the pope); the issue of language

(Greek versus Latin), particularly in its use in the liturgy (the Mass); and political ambitions of those entrusted with the spiritual leadership of the church.

The split may have been averted had it not been for two individuals who were driven more by ambition than by their spiritual callings. Humbert of Silva Candida was a French Benedictine abbot and later a cardinal. He and Bruno (later to become Leo IX) had become friends and allies, as both were very interested in spiritual and political reforms in the church. When Bruno was made pope, Humbert was made archbishop of Sicily in 1050. Humbert was a gifted Greek and Latin scholar and vigorously defended the exclusive use of Latin in the church. He authored a work, *Adversus Graecorum Calumnias* (*Against the Slanders of the Greeks*),[48] that particularly argued against issues advanced by Michael Cerularius, the patriarch of Constantinople.

In fairness, although it's rarely mentioned in history books, Patriarch Michael Cerularius was extremely ambitious. He was described as "arrogant and overbearing,"[49] and while the charge can easily be made that all too often the Roman popes were too involved in secular matters, a similar charge can be made of Cerularius, who not only had imperial ambitions but also saw himself as superior to the other three Eastern patriarchs of Jerusalem, Antioch, and Alexandria.[50]

Unfortunately Cardinal Humbert had similar personality and leadership flaws when Pope Leo IX sent him to Constantinople with a charge to determine the opportunity of a Greek-Latin reunion proposed by Eastern Emperor Constantine IX. Instead of looking for opportunities to resolve differences in the liturgy, celibacy, and language, and the often-mentioned three-word change in the Nicene Creed (*Filioque*, Latin for "and the Son"), Humbert frustrated his Greek hosts, lost his patience, and marched into the cathedral of Hagia Sophia on July 16, 1054, and officially excommunicated Patriarch Michael Cerularius.

Cerularius reciprocated and excommunicated both Cardinal Humbert and Pope Leo IX, who had actually died a few months prior. Neither Cerularius (who refused to meet personally with Humbert) nor the cardinal were interested in the unity of the church for which Pope

Leo IX had hoped. It wasn't until the Second Vatican Council in 1965 that these excommunications were overturned, restoring Communion but not unity in the church.

The remaining three patriarchs of Alexandria, Jerusalem, and Antioch ultimately sided with Constantinople in the split and are considered Orthodox to this day. However, because of the split and the fortune of history, the Orthodox Church never had its equivalent Protestant Reformation. While there remain many similarities between the Eastern Orthodox Church and the Roman Catholic Church, to this day these Orthodox patriarchs do not consider themselves the heads of the church (that would be Jesus Christ) but as patriarchs and servants of the church.

CHAPTER TWENTY-FOUR

The Western Schism

Two Popes Bad...Three Popes Even Worse

Main entrance of the Palais des Papes in Avignon, France,
which became the official residence of the popes in AD
1309. Photographic reproduction in the public domain.

Recently we saw a very unusual event. In February 2013 Pope Benedict XVI resigned. He had served since his election as pope in 2005, when he had succeeded the ever-popular John Paul II (John Paul the Great).

Even casual observers of world events knew it was unusual for a pope to resign. Historians quickly told us that while it was not completely without precedent, it had been almost six hundred years since it had happened—in AD 1415, when Pope Gregory XII had resigned at the end of one of the most tumultuous periods in the history of the church, known as the Western Schism.

The Western Schism had a number of components but is most often defined as the time between AD 1378 and AD 1417, when the Roman Catholic Church had rival popes and headquarters in Avignon, France, and Rome, Italy.

The causes and origins of the Western Schism are many, but the best explanation was the decay and collapse of Rome itself. By the middle of the fourteenth century, Rome was a mess. Since the fall of the Roman Empire and the murder of the last Western Roman emperor in AD 480, Rome had been sacked, set on fire, vandalized, and subsidized. The flow of pilgrims from all over Europe was a source of income, and Rome always had its spiritual prominence but paled in comparison to other city-states in Europe.

A number of pontiffs entered dangerous and unwise alliances with political leaders in Europe, often picking the wrong guy in regional conflicts and power struggles. The result was typically not good for Rome, as the city and the people were often punished. The citizens of Rome often rebelled, and mob rule left scars, burned buildings, and a further lack of prestige for both the city of Rome and the papacy.

A number of events in Europe had weakened the authority of the church in general and the pope specifically. In particular the Black Death, also known as the bubonic plague, had broken out in China in the early 1330s, and it only took a few years for merchants in ships to bring the plague to Europe.

Neither medieval medicine nor the power of the church was able to stop the plague. Over the centuries people had developed almost a superstitious belief in the power of the church. The cross, holy water, the Communion table, and the touch of the priest were all things that would merit not only spiritual blessings but temporal blessings as well. Many in the church taught that the good prospered while those who were evil were punished not only in the next world but in the present.

Between AD 1347 and AD 1349, it is believed that as many as 60 percent of those in Europe died.[51] The plague struck young and old, rich and poor, priest and penitent. Initially many looked to the church and the pope for help, but it became obvious very quickly that the church could do nothing to stop the advance of the plague. While we know today that it was a bacterium, a bacillus, that spread the plague through the air, in water, and through the bites of both fleas and rats, at the time the plague seemed like an act of God.

Whether the plague came from God or nature, it was obvious to the people that the church was powerless against its advance. While some at the time became more devout, others who escaped the plague took on a carefree "enjoy today, for tomorrow we may die" attitude. Many abandoned their previous religious way of life that to them was no longer meaningful, giving in to temptations and vice. Perhaps the English poet William Langland, a contemporary of the famous Geoffrey Chaucer, best summarized the opinions of millions when he wrote, "Prayers have no power to hinder these plagues. For God is deaf nowadays and deigns not to hear us."[52]

While the plague was a contributing factor in the circumstances that preceded the Western Schism, it was the dilapidated, ruined, and literally smelly city of Rome that caused the newly elected Pope Clement V in AD 1305 to have reason to move the pope's residence from Rome to Avignon, France. Clement had been elected primarily because of the support of French King Philip the Fair, who had stacked the deck with French cardinals who would elect French popes.

The move to Avignon lasted for nearly seventy years, from AD 1309 to AD 1377. While some good came out of the reigns of the seven French popes, including reforms among the clergy, expanded missionary efforts, and a promotion of education, the alignment of the papacy with the kingdom of France and the antagonistic relationships with the neighboring kingdoms of Spain, Germany, and England damaged the already diminished prestige of the papacy.

The seventh French pope of Avignon was Pope Gregory XI, who returned to Rome in AD 1377 but died the next year. Roman mobs, concerned that another French pope would return to Avignon, broke into the cardinal enclave and insisted on an Italian-born pope. The cardinals gave in to the mob and voted in Urban VI. Urban soon proved to be an unwise choice and quickly became so unpopular that within months, the cardinals gathered again to elect another pope—Clement VII, who took up residence in Avignon with a competing cardinal curia, administration, and court.

With the election of Clement VII, the Western Schism had begun, and from AD 1378 to AD 1418 there would be a person calling himself the pope and the legitimate successor of Peter the apostle in both Rome and Avignon.

That takes us back to the earlier mention of Pope Gregory XII, whom a conclave in Rome elected in AD 1406 to be the pope, with an arrangement that both Gregory XII and the rival pope, Benedict XIII of Avignon, would resign and allow a fresh election to end the Western Schism.

While church historians believe this was Pope Gregory XII's earnest desire, when the cardinals gathered together and elected Alexander V, neither Gregory XII nor Benedict XIII resigned, and the church had three popes, each claiming the throne of Peter the Apostle.

Finally the Council of Constance (1414–1418) ended the three-pope confusion. Pope Gregory played an important role in the council and again offered his resignation in order for the cardinals to elect a new pope. The council deposed the recent popes of Avignon as antipopes, declared Pope Gregory the cardinal bishop of Porto, and elected a new pope, Martin V, finally ending the Western Schism.

While the Council of Constance was able to bring unity back to the Roman Catholic Church, this was the same council that also unfortunately condemned both John Wyclif of England and John Hus of Bohemia. These two pre-Luther reformers in the church had very large followings and advocated many of the reforms that would soon launch the Protestant Reformation.

The Council of Constance summoned John Hus to Constance, and the emperor assured Hus of safe conduct while at the council. At the same time the council was planning on burning him at the stake as a heretic. The people of Constance cheered when John Hus arrived, but the pastor, educator, and theologian was soon arrested, convicted, and burned at the stake. When the executioner stoked the fire, John Hus was heard to say, "What I taught with my lips I now seal with my blood."[53]

The fires of the Reformation had already begun with both Wyclif and Hus. One hundred years later, and unlike other early reformers and revivalists, Martin Luther and his teaching would survive and change the history of the church.

CHAPTER TWENTY-FIVE

Revivals and Prelude to the Reformation

What Really Happened in 1492?

The Capitulation of Granada by Francisco Pradilla y Ortiz
(1848–1921), showing Muhammad XII confronting
Ferdinand and Isabella. Location: Palacio del Senado de
España (Madrid, Spain). Photographic reproduction and
original work in the public domain.

Roaming Catholics

I was actually a pretty good student, and the nuns at St. Joseph's school were good teachers. While many of my friends who attended Catholic school relate stories about smacks on the knuckles with rulers and flying erasers (the average nun's aim and accuracy at twenty meters with an eraser was remarkable), I choose to remember the actual education. Spelling was at the bottom for me, but literature, mathematics, geography, and religion classes were all interesting, and I did well. History was my favorite, as it was much more than dates and events; it was also people and tragedy, kings and countries, armies, battles, and wars.

I loved American history but was attracted as well to European history. The textbooks at the time were much more patriotic than today. History hadn't been rewritten, and George Washington was still a great man, not just a Virginian slaveholder. Along the way we also learned about ancient Greece and the Roman Empire and, of course, Christopher Columbus.

So here is a trick question: What happened in 1492? OK, maybe this isn't a trick question, but from the perspective of this chapter and a very important event in church history, there was an event in 1492 other than Christopher Columbus and his voyage to the New World. Interestingly it also involved Ferdinand and Isabella. In 1492 the combined forces of King Ferdinand V of Aragon and Queen Isabella I of Castile finally conquered the Moorish kingdom of Granada in Southern Spain.

Ferdinand and Isabella had been married in 1469 in an arranged marriage while they were yet teenagers. The marriage brought unity and stability under what ended up becoming two very capable administrators. The kingdoms of Aragon and Castile, while maintaining their own identities for the next few decades, finally in 1492 were able to embrace the large territory of Granada. These united kingdoms and a united people entered into what historians refer to as Spain's *El Siglo de Oro*, or the Golden Age of Spain.

The struggle with the Moors had been going on for seven centuries. The Moors had crossed the Strait of Gibraltar in AD 711 and had pushed the Christian kings and their armies back into Southern France by AD 1300. At one point Christianity was in severe distress, with the Moors dominating Northern Africa and in the west conquering Spain. In the east the Arabs and Turks conquered Constantinople in 1453 and pushed in as far as Venice, Italy.

In 1492, however, with the Moors pushed out of Spain, Ferdinand and Isabella turned their attention toward the unity of their kingdoms, and they decided that one of the best ways to bring unity was through Christianity. For centuries the Iberian Peninsula had large Muslim and Jewish populations, and through the years this diversity had contributed greatly to the culture, including the arts, architecture, language, and fashion. The Moors had established great universities and had incredible scholars.

The Spanish Inquisition had officially started in 1478, after the *reyes Católicos*—as the Catholic monarchs, Ferdinand and Isabella, were called—pressured Pope Sixtus IV into allowing them to have complete and exclusive control of the ecclesiastical tribunal. This authority included the naming of the grand inquisitors, who were accountable to no one except the monarchs.

The Spanish Inquisition forced many of the Jews and Muslims to convert. However, many remained faithful to their religion, and converts were often challenged—therefore, the persecution continued. In 1492 local church leaders persuaded the *reyes Católicos* finally to expel all of the Jews.

While tens of thousands of Jews and Moors had agreed to be baptized to avoid persecution, historians believe many were tortured and executed. This included not only the Jews and Moors who had converted in name only but also Christians who were conveniently accused of heresy when they were more likely economic and political enemies of powerful people in the church and government.

By the beginning of the sixteenth century, the flames of revival had begun, and the new Gutenberg printing press quickly spread the teachings of people like John Wyclif, John Tyndale, and John Hus as well as Peter Waldo of France.

All of these pre-Luther reformers were actually revivalists who were deeply committed Christians. They were well educated, typically scholars and priests, and individually had become convinced that the Catholic

Church's teachings had departed from much of what scripture taught. They typically believed that the Bible should be accessible in the common language, stressed personal faith, and took issue with the church's wealth and power.

While it was very possible the Spirit of God was moving in the hearts of the people, and Europe was experiencing a rebirth of literature, the arts, philosophy, and science, many of the leaders of the church, and particularly those in power, such as Ferdinand and Isabella, doubled down on insisting on universal conformity to the traditions, teachings, and power of the Catholic Church. For centuries the unity of the church had been accomplished by forcing everyone to conform to the customs, traditions, and teachings of those in power. Questioning the authority of the curia and even preaching the Gospel outside of official activities sanctioned by the church would bring quick reprisal, persecution, and often martyrdom.

CHAPTER TWENTY-SIX

Rebuild My Church

St. Francis of Assisi

Fresco. Giotto Di Bondone, circa 1298. *Legend of St. Francis: 15. Sermon to the Birds.* Location: Basilique Assise in Italy. Photographic reproduction and original work in the public domain.

The prophetic words "Rebuild my church" and the accepted start date of the Protestant Reformation were actually separated by more than three hundred years. However, to understand fully the cause, reasons, and results of the Protestant Reformation, we have to go back to the beginning of the thirteenth century and the calling of St. Francis of Assisi.

We know a great deal about St. Francis of Assisi. He was an unlikely saint, and an unlikely reformer of the church. Francis was the son of a wealthy Italian cloth merchant. Like many fathers, his had dreams that Francis would not only be interested in the family business but would also prove to be a gallant and brave knight. Francis did what he considered his obligatory military training but was captured when his hometown of Assisi declared war on its longtime enemy, Perugia. Young Francis was imprisoned for a year.

In prison Francis read the New Testament and was captivated by the Gospel accounts of Jesus and the radical teachings of service, sacrifice, and dedication. After his release from prison, he returned home to Assisi but wanted to dedicate his life to these teachings of Jesus. One day, while spending time in prayer in a chapel in San Damiano, just outside of Assisi, he heard a voice seeming to come from the crucifix: "Francis, go rebuild my church, which you see is falling into ruins."[54]

Francis was overjoyed that the Lord would speak to him. He went to his father's warehouse. He admitted later to stealing some cloth and selling it to buy bricks, as he literally wanted to do as the Lord had said: to rebuild the church at San Damiano. Later Francis was reading the story of the rich, young ruler. Jesus's words—"Sell what you have, give it to the poor, and come follow me"[55]—gave Francis further purpose.

Again believing that Jesus was speaking directly to him through the Gospel account, Francis decided to turn his back on the world and devote his life to fasting and prayer.

When his father and the local parish priest confronted Francis about the theft of the cloth, Francis took off his fine clothes and threw them at his father, renouncing his inheritance and declaring his loyalty to God alone. It was reported that he said to his father, "Until now, I called you father. From now on, my only father is my Father in heaven."[56]

Francis fashioned some clothing from a burlap bag and a rope he took from a scarecrow. In a short amount of time, he became a cult figure, attracting at first few followers. He would beg from the rich, give to the poor, and preach the Gospel to everyone. Soon huge crowds would gather in both the towns and countryside.

Francis was radical. The church of the twelfth and thirteenth centuries was suffering from greed, corruption, and scandal. Wealthy families purchased most high church offices at the time, and all too often even the pope was more concerned with political alliances and going after the enemies of his friends than advancing the kingdom of God.

Francis, while not sanctioned by the church, began his ministry to the common people and preached sermons in common Latin (not ecclesiastical or church Latin). He avoided the parish churches and taught the Gospel to the common man in barns, in the countryside, and on the village streets.

When St. Francis went to Rome to ask for the recognition of his monastic order, Pope Innocent III refused to see him and reportedly told him to go "lie down with the pigs."[57]

Surprisingly St. Francis returned after an extended absence, stinking like pigs. As a result Pope Innocent III agreed to his request and is credited with recognizing the Franciscan order. We often see Francis pictured with birds and other animals, as it was told that he would preach the Gospel even to them as he traveled.

Francis died on October 3, 1226. Afterward it was said of him: "For a few years, the Sermon on the Mount became a realized fact. But the dream passed."[58]

Many church historians believe that while the Catholic Church was fighting bloody Crusades and administering the Inquisition, St. Francis of Assisi was preaching peace and love. His message led to Catholic Church reforms and delayed the Protestant Reformation for almost three hundred years.

CHAPTER TWENTY-SEVEN

The Protestant Reformation

The Righteous Will Live by Faith

Portrait of Martin Luther as an Augustine Monk by Lucas
Cranach the Elder, circa 1546. Location: Germanisches
National museum in Nuremberg, Germany. Photographic
reproduction and original work in the public domain.

In the two centuries after the death of St. Francis, all of the structure, doctrines, and teachings of the Catholic Church would be fully developed and would give rise ultimately to the Protestant Reformation. As we have discussed, these teachings and doctrines developed over time, some taking centuries and some actually embraced only then to be reversed by later popes. By 1517, the official beginning of the Reformation, all of Western Europe was divided by the Catholic Church into geographic dioceses and archdioceses. The Catholic papacy was strong and had the support of nations and kings. In addition, the church was powerful and had great wealth, primarily concentrated in land that nobility and wealthy landowners and merchants had donated over the centuries.

A present-day Roman Catholic would find that the major doctrines and the sacraments of the Latin Church prior to the time of the Reformation were substantially the same as those presently acknowledged by the Roman Catholic Church. However, this would not be true of the culture of the church, as the common teachings and depictions of God, purgatory, and hell (three very common topics of the time) would shock most modern-day Roman Catholics. The God of the late Middle Ages and into the time of the Renaissance was depicted as vindictive, vengeful, and judgmental. There was very little love, joy, and mercy in the common teachings of the era, and both hell and purgatory were common images that were both frightening and motivating.

While it is not unusual today for some preachers to choose the fire and brimstone approach while others focus on a loving and merciful God, the church of the Middle Ages was much more of the former than the latter. Fire and brimstone were also its references to time in purgatory, not an eternity in hell. The common teaching of the time was that Catholics, because they were baptized, could go to heaven if they avoided very serious sin but were certain to spend an undetermined amount of time in purgatory, which was always described in terms that were equal to or even worse than today's more horrific descriptions of hell. The only difference between purgatory and hell, according to the teachings of the church, was that purgatory was temporary even if it lasted a few thousand years. In addition, there was only one exit from purgatory, and it was also an entrance to heaven—delayed as a result of a lifetime's accumulation of sins, but heaven nevertheless.

The sins of the individual did not entirely determine the time spent in purgatory. The church of the Middle Ages claimed it possessed a Treasury of Merit, accumulated by saints who earned more merit than they needed to enter heaven. Sinners, both those living as well as the departed, could tap in to this treasury to secure their early release.

While we covered the teaching regarding purgatory thoroughly in chapter 18, the Treasury of Merit is the key teaching that supported the dual foundation of both purgatory and the sale of indulgences, which gained popularity in the fifteenth century. This arrangement was a win-win for the sinner and the church as indulgences provided time off of the obligatory period one would spend in purgatory and served as a type of Middle Ages capital campaign.

Between Dante's depiction of Mount Purgatory in his fourteenth-century epic *Divine Comedy* and the parish priest's teaching, purgatory was depicted as a horrible place of torment, punishment, hellfire, despair, and anguish. This teaching greatly impacted individuals' opinions of God. They viewed themselves as lowly and sinful and unable to satisfy the demands of a vengeful God without the assistance of the church. This reinforced and elevated the importance of the local church, the sacraments, and the priesthood.

Such was the religious teaching and the culture in the church when young Martin Luther (born Martinus Luder in 1483) abruptly abandoned his studies of the law and ultimately became a priest. The story is told that Luther, while already finished with his legal studies (he had received his master's degree at age twenty-one), was nearly struck by lightning, and, fearing death, he vowed to become a monk.

From his childhood Martin had been plagued by thoughts that he was spiritually inadequate. His thinking was reinforced by the harsh punishment he received from his parents and at school. His image of God as vengeful and judgmental compounded his feelings of inadequacy. He was convinced that his parents' corporal punishment was a precursor to even more torment in the afterlife in purgatory because of his sinfulness.

Young Martin entered an Augustinian monastery in Erfurt, Germany, to the north of Nuremberg, in 1505 and took his vow as a monk the next year. The Augustinian monks were known for their self-discipline, devotion, and sacrifice, and Martin rose to the occasion. Later Martin Luther wrote of this early life, "I kept the rule of my order so strictly that if ever a monk got to heaven by his monkery, it was I."[59]

His feelings of inadequacy persisted, and Luther would spend hours confessing his sins and transgressions to God and his superiors. He wrote of this time, "I was myself more than once driven to the very depths of despair so that I wished I had never been created. Love God? I hated him!...I lost touch with Christ the Savior and Comforter, and made of him the jailor and hangman of my poor soul."[60]

Martin Luther's superiors at the monastery recognized him for his keen intellect and knowledge of Latin and gave him the opportunity to study theology at the university. In 1507, at the age of twenty-three, he became a priest. The following year Martin was given a prestigious teaching assignment at the University of Wittenberg.

Most scholars point to two events that greatly influenced Martin Luther and his loyalty and confidence in the hierarchy of the church. After these events he would become a very thoughtful and articulate critic of some of the teachings and traditions that had been formulated over centuries.

The first event was a pilgrimage that Martin Luther and another Augustinian monk were sent on in 1510 to Rome, the Eternal City. Their objective was to visit and further build their faith as well as conduct some official business regarding rules in the Augustinian order. The visit did not endear the twenty-six-year-old Luther to Rome or its ecclesiastical occupants and church rulers. While he accomplished the things any faithful pilgrim would do, Martin saw what he believed to be the wholesale corruption in the higher offices of the church, including the papacy. He was also highly skeptical of the medieval relics and artifacts that were often for sale or available to view for a price.

The second event is well known to historians and Protestants. It is known as the posting of the Ninety-Five Theses, or challenges, on the door of the castle church at Wittenberg, Germany. His theses had the official title of "Disputation on the Power and Efficacy of Indulgences Commonly Known as The 95 Theses," and he posted them on October 31, 1517, nearly five hundred years ago.

Martin Luther at the time was highly respected, with a doctorate in theology. While he was only thirty-four years old, throughout Germany he had become a well-known scholar and lecturer. He was in charge of eleven area Augustinian monasteries and was also a professor at the university. He served additionally as the parish priest at Wittenberg.

Approximately one year prior to his posting of the famous—or infamous—Ninety-Five Theses, he had published *Theologia Germanica* (*German Theology*), which was based on an earlier fourteenth-century work. The theology book proposed a Christian life based on the example of Jesus Christ, a renunciation of sin and selfishness, and a close union with God by following a spiritual and disciplined path of prayer and study.

Also in the same year, 1516, Luther had what historians refer to as his tower experience. In doing research for his *Theologia Germanica*, he was drawn to the writings of St. Augustine, the great theologian of the fourth century. Luther related later that the tower experience was the major turning point in his life.

Luther was in prayer and study and was reading Paul's letter to the Romans, chapter 1:17: "For in the gospel a righteousness from God is revealed, a righteousness that is by faith from first to last, just as it is written 'The righteous will live by faith.'" This was the same verse Augustine had wrestled with more than a millennium earlier. Martin had read the verse many times before, but this time it was an epiphany. All of his life, he had been tormented by feelings of inadequacy and feared God's judgment. This verse, however, revealed that all of the fasting and self-deprecation, the hours of confession in order to earn salvation, counted for nothing.

This verse in Romans for both Luther and Augustine revealed that salvation was unmerited—a true gift of God's grace. Regarding his reflection on Romans 1:17, Luther stated, "I felt I was altogether born again… That place in Paul was truly my gate to paradise."[61]

The timing of Luther's epiphany was important. At nearly the same time, the newly appointed archbishop in Germany, Albrecht of Mainz, received permission from Pope Leo X to authorize Johann Tetzel, a German Dominican friar, to sell indulgences to the German populace for the rebuilding of St. Peter's Basilica in Rome. The proceeds, according to historians of the period, were to be split fifty-fifty. Rome would receive one half, and one half went toward the repayment of a loan the archbishop owed to a wealthy family who had loaned him money to purchase the office of archbishop. This practice of purchasing high church offices was very widespread in the Middle Ages and was called simony, after Simon in the book of Acts, whom the apostle Paul condemned for wanting to purchase the power of the Holy Spirit.

It was reported that Tetzel created a chart that listed prices for various types of sins and the time taken off a soul's time in purgatory.

Martin Luther firmly believed that the selling of indulgences was sinful and an obvious example of wholesale corruption in the church that started at the very top, with the pope.

Many historians and theologians agree that Martin Luther had no intention of starting a denomination but desired reforms within the church. He, like many who preceded him, began to articulate challenges to the teaching, practices, and even the theology of the church. His attacks, while appearing to be public, were addressed to the leadership of the church, very intentionally including the pope. Most people aren't aware that Martin Luther wrote the Ninety-Five Theses in ecclesiastical Latin, a language that few besides the educated church clergy would understand. Also, nailing commentary, arguments, or a thesis to a church door was a common practice; church doors were often used like contemporary community bulletin boards

In these Ninety-Five Theses, Martin Luther charged that the indulgences had no power to forgive sin nor to remit the time in purgatory. He criticized the power of the pope and the extreme wealth of the church. He criticized in particular Tetzel's saying, "As soon as a coin in the coffer rings, the rescued soul from purgatory springs."[62] Luther challenged the concept of the Treasury of Merit, saying there was neither a biblical basis nor ample church tradition.

Luther's theses immediately stimulated discussion among university intellectuals. Timing is everything! Because of the invention of the printing press, his theses as well as his articles and arguments were published and widely distributed across Europe.

For years intellectuals, clergy, and laypeople alike had been skeptical of the upper echelon of the church hierarchy. Since the return of the papacy to Rome after what Martin Luther and others would later refer to as the Babylonian captivity of the church, when as many as three men claimed the office of the papacy at the same time, the respect for both the office of the pope and the inhabitants of the office had been tarnished. In addition scholars, clergy, and laypeople alike had a growing disdain for the growing army of high church office holders and bureaucrats.

It was, however, the abuse of power, the selling of indulgences, the corruption of the bishops, the excesses of the church curia, and the political posturing of both the secular and religious rulers that ultimately created enough uproar that the Roman church could no longer effectively extinguish the passion and preaching of the reformers.

Some of the forerunners of Martin Luther were brilliant, holy, and passionate men. These pre-Reformation leaders included Peter Waldo (1140–1217), who held the Bible as the foundation of the faith and rejected lavish lifestyles of the church leaders; John Wyclif (1328–1384), an Oxford scholar who translated the New Testament into English; John Hus (1369–1415), a Czech Catholic priest who emphasized the role of scripture in determining life and doctrine; and Girolamo Savonarola (1452–1498), an Italian Dominican friar who called for higher moral standards and railed against church largess.

After Martin Luther's successful reformation of the church in Germany, other reformers, such as John Calvin of France, Huldrych Zwingli of Switzerland, and John Knox of Scotland, embraced many of his teachings. The common denominator among these reformers and the basis of the Protestant Reformation was that salvation was a gift from God and not a result of works; the authority of the Bible was greater than the authority of the pope; and the rejection of an exclusive sacramental priesthood, teaching instead that all believers were part of a holy priesthood.

Martin Luther was quite modest in his changes in the culture of the church, avoiding extreme change lest it become too confusing for the masses. Other reformers, both contemporary and later, typically built upon Luther's success and, taking the Bible as their guidebook, began to disassemble infant baptism, the liturgy, the clergy, and the episcopate (the ruling authority of the church).

While the prophetic words "Rebuild my church," which St. Francis of Assisi heard, and the accepted start date of the Protestant Reformation were separated by more than three hundred years, some of the causes, reasons, and results of both reforms had profound impacts on a church that now, in both its East and West traditions, as well as its Roman and Protestant traditions, includes more than two billion adherents.

CHAPTER TWENTY-EIGHT

The Catholic Counter-Reformation

The New World and Religious Liberty

Council of Trent by Pasquale Cati da Jesi, 1588, Location:
the Basilica of Our Lady in Trastevere, Rome, Italy.
Photographic reproduction and original work in the
public domain.

Martin Luther was not the first Catholic priest, monk, friar, or theologian to call for changes in the church, nor was he responsible for the first split in the church. In AD 1054 the church had split into East and West, and in reality the bishop of Rome, also known as the pope, had separated himself from the traditional and geographical ruling group of five patriarchs. The pope was no longer one leader among five but the one and only ruler. The other four patriarchs continued without interruption their unique worship styles, customs, and liturgies and shared leadership of what would become the Orthodox Church.

After Martin Luther's public display on October 31, 1517, of complaints or charges against the pope and some of the abuses and his criticism of the sale of indulgences, and due to the relatively recent invention of the printing press, Luther's teachings became the talk of Germany and much of Europe.

After his postings of the Ninety-Five Theses, the Office of the Inquisition of the Catholic Church summoned Luther to immediately appear in Rome to answer charges of heresy. Unlike other reformers who were summoned to Rome and typically martyred, Luther had a protector in Frederick the Wise of Saxony (Germany) and chose not to go to Rome. Instead he began a series of lectures on the book of Hebrews. During this time his teachings continued to gather broad support among the common people as well as nobility and landowners.

The reasons for Luther's support were varied. Many believe it was a revival, spurred by the Holy Spirit, that brought necessary reforms to the church. For others it was fueled by economic and political reasons. In my opinion it was clearly both. Luther continued his criticism and, over a few years, dug deeper into issues, which included primarily four topics: the priesthood, the scriptures, the gift of grace, and the process of justification.

Four years after the nailing of the Ninety-Five Theses, Pope Leo X excommunicated Luther, and in the same year Roman emperor Charles V ordered Luther to appear before him at what is now called the Diet of Worms in Germany.

Martin Luther's protector, Frederick the Wise, promised safe passage, and when Luther traveled to Worms, the populace in each city on his journey greeted him as a hero. When the inquisitors at Worms accused him, he bravely defended each point of his attacks on traditional Catholic belief, the power of the pope, and the role of scripture versus Catholic tradition and continually refused to recant. He concluded his testimony by stating:

> Unless I am convinced by the testimony of the Scriptures or by clear reason (for I do not trust either in the pope or in councils alone, since it is well known that they have often erred and contradicted themselves), I am bound by the Scriptures I have quoted and my conscience is captive to the Word of God. I cannot and will not recant anything, since it is neither safe nor right to go against conscience. May God help me. Amen.[63]

The final ruling by Emperor Charles V declared that Martin Luther was a heretic and an outlaw. However, because of his popularity with the people, the emperor never tried to have him arrested. Just to be safe, Martin spent the better part of a couple of years in seclusion at Wartburg Castle. There he spent much time in study and translated the Bible into German from the ancient Hebrew and Greek texts.

Within a few years, the reformers mentioned in the previous chapter, including John Calvin of France, Huldrych Zwingli of Switzerland, and John Knox of Scotland, were joined by what have been called other radical reformers who believed that Luther and the others had not gone far enough in their reforms and encouraged even more profound changes, including (but not all agreeing on) teachings regarding a complete separation from the state, literal biblicism, pacifism, and adult baptism. This was called the Anabaptist movement.

Three more popes would be elected before Cardinal Alessandro Farnese of Italy was elected to the papacy in 1534 and took the name Pope Paul III. By that time Protestantism had spread throughout

Europe, England had experienced a reformation, and King Henry VIII had established the Church of England. The Catholic Church and the pope's absolute rule in the spiritual lives of the people had ended. Nearly half of the population of Europe was no longer united under the banner of Catholicism and referred to those who still followed the rule of the pope as Roman Catholics, an intentional pejorative, as many of the names for various Christian denominations would have been in their original meanings.

Many historians think Pope Paul III was an unlikely candidate to call for reforms within the Catholic Church in general and the power of the curia (the pope, pontifical legates, councils, and secretaries) in particular. The pope came from the Farnese family, a wealthy and powerful family that had previously produced Pope Boniface VIII. He was appointed cardinal at age twenty-five and had a mistress for many years with whom he fathered three sons and a daughter. He was ordained as a priest in 1519, twenty-six years after becoming a cardinal, and when he was elected pope his first orders were to elevate his two grandsons to the office of cardinal at ages fourteen and sixteen, respectively.[64]

Nevertheless, Pope Paul III had a change of heart and lifestyle and approached his ministry with a heart toward reform. In 1536 he appointed a committee to address various issues of abuse in the curia, abuses within church administration, and the lack of formal education in the priesthood. He proposed appointing a joint ecumenical council to address these and other issues, but his cardinals objected. Normally the pope would have prevailed, but wars in France, Spain, and Italy as well as attacks by the Turks delayed any formal meetings for years.

Finally, in 1545, the church convened the Council of Trent in the town of Trento, Italy. This council would actually last through three popes, three individual sessions, and finally was concluded in 1563. There was little effort to achieve actual reconciliation with the Protestants, who by that time represented many different and varied theological teachings. The Council of Trent defended traditional Roman Catholic teachings regarding the church, the role of priesthood, and the role of tradition.

The council rejected the reformers' teachings regarding the doctrines of grace and justification. Most importantly for the Roman Catholic Church, the council affirmed and clearly defined modern Roman Catholic teaching on transubstantiation, the Mass, veneration of saints, sacred tradition, and original sin.

Unfortunately the lack of reconciliation between these now distinct and divergent branches of Christianity and the strong bond between church and state led to the Thirty Years' War in central Europe from 1618 to 1648. The previous centuries of hostility and war in Europe clearly illustrated that the kings, rulers, monarchs, and even church rulers were very quick to draw the sword for varied reasons. The Thirty Years' War was similar in that it was fought for a combination of political, economic, opportunistic, and religious passions. It was one of the most devastating and longest-lasting military conflicts in Europe, with as many as eleven million people dying as a result of military action or because of the resulting famine and disease. More than fifteen nations were involved, and the geographic, economic, and military balance of Europe was forever changed.

During that time, however, a new world had been discovered and colonized by the European nations. The religious persecution, war, and religious hostilities of the Old World had a huge impact on the new settlements in the New World. Beginning with the Pilgrims, who came to the New World in 1620, and continuing with the immigration of Puritans, who were separatists from the Church of England, many of the immigrants to the New World had very strong religious beliefs. In Central and South America, Spain and Portugal took the lead and established the Roman Catholic faith among the indigenous people as well as the new immigrants. In North America waves of Anglicans, Dutch Calvinists, English Puritans, French Catholics and Huguenots, German Lutherans, and assorted Anabaptists, Quakers, Moravians, and Jews had huge impacts on the spiritual culture of the settlements and profound impacts on the Bill of Rights, which was ratified in 1791. Those seeking religious freedom were successful in establishing revolutionary ideas related to the freedom of assembly and religion in the founding of the United States of America. Protestants were the obvious majority in much of the colonial United States, and the Roman Catholic Church had huge gains in Central and South America and in the end had more than three times the geographic territory it had lost to Protestantism in Europe.

Christianity in the United States, from its founding until arguably just recently, was the most important cultural component in everyday life. Christianity had a profound influence and was the common moral agent in the establishment of law, the court systems, the understanding of due process, and equality. Interestingly it was the establishment of the First Amendment to the United States Constitution, granting freedom of religion, that created the opportunity not only for the spread of Christianity but also the growth of diverse and often competing Protestant denominations and subgroups.

The Pilgrims may have had the initial idea of living in a country where they could freely worship their God without interference from European churches or political enemies, but it was the Christian revivals, known as the First and the Second Great Awakenings of the 1730s and 1790s, that led to the strong Evangelical and holiness movements in America. These religious revivals not only brought people back into the churches but also spawned dozens of new Christian Protestant denominations that were no longer tied to their European counterparts but were clearly American in their theological understanding and in their governance, which was often very democratic or congregational in nature.

Catholic and Protestant Christians have coexisted peacefully in the United States, with few exceptions, for most of our history. However, peaceful coexistence is a poor substitute for true acceptance or tolerance, let alone unity.

The Roman Catholic Church for years has made efforts not only toward reform but also ecumenism. While many are suspicious, Pope Francis has made efforts toward dialogue and even reconciliation with American Evangelicals and Pentecostals. It may be that the reason Pope

Francis has reached out toward these Christian groups rather than the historic denominational groups is both that these groups tend to be more conservative with regard to traditional Christian moral beliefs and that these groups are growing, compared to diminishing numbers in the main-line Protestant denominations.

CHAPTER TWENTY-NINE

Embrace the Wonder

As soon as all the people saw Jesus, they were overwhelmed with wonder and ran to greet him.
—Mark 9:15

Suffer the Little Children. Stained glass windows by Paul Woodroff, circa 1902. Location: St Ethelbert's church in Herringswell, Suffolk, England. Photographic reproduction and original work in the public domain.

O ver the past two thousand years, the church has grown from a small group of only 120 on Pentecost to more than two billion people, or about one third of the entire world population. The words of Jesus in Matthew 16:18 that the gates of hell will not prevail against it have certainly been true.

After learning about the history, the teachings, and the development of the doctrines of the church, I would encourage the reader to end the wandering and that now is the time to embrace the wonder. Jesus is the Son of God. He came, was born of the Virgin, lived, died, and rose from the dead, just as the scriptures say.

The early Christians fully embraced the teachings of Jesus. They were filled with the Holy Spirit on the day of Pentecost and scattered to spread the Gospel. Many were martyred for their faith, as they lived in a world that was hostile to the message of forgiveness, redemption, and resurrection.

One of my seminary professors, teaching the Gospel of Mark, called it the book of wonder. The Greek word *thambeō*, which is translated as "astonished, to be amazed or wonder" occurs thirty-two times in the book of Mark. In Mark's Gospel account, people were *amazed* when they saw the man who was paralyzed get up and walk (Mark 2:12); they were *astonished* when Jesus calmed the wind and the waves (Mark 6:51); and when the deaf man was able to hear and speak (Mark 7:37). The disciples were full of *wonder* when Jesus told them about the kingdom of God (Mark 10:32).

We simply need to embrace the wonder; we don't have to try to explain it. While we may not be able to rationalize it, we believe that Jesus is the Christ, the Son of God. We confess that He rose from the dead and that He will come again in glory.

We wonder because we too are amazed. We wonder because Jesus, the eternal Son of God, came to earth in order to die for our sins. We wonder because we are told that forgiveness is available and that God gives His grace freely to us when we open our hearts to Jesus. We are amazed at the ability of God's Holy Spirit to change our hearts and our minds and make us new creations.

All too often people want to believe, but they have wandered away. They don't necessarily have any issue with the essential teachings about Jesus. They have no reason to disbelieve the Bible. They believe that Jesus was born of the Virgin, that He died and rose again. However, their local church or the entire denomination—Catholic, Orthodox, or Protestant—has disappointed them. They are disappointed, so they leave.

It's the job of the church leaders to not disappoint. The apostle Paul warned them that their calling was critically important. They were to be pastors, which is the translation of the word shepherd. The pastor's job was to protect, to minister, to comfort, to instruct, and to preach. They are to be an example and are held to a higher standard because they have a higher purpose. One of their primary purposes is to teach that we are to be one in Christ.

However, for much of the two thousand years, schisms, divisions, dissensions, and even full-blown apostasy have shaken the church. These schisms, divisions, and dissensions have distracted the church from its primary mission to make disciples and baptize them in the name of Jesus.[65] Jesus prayed that the church may be one just as He and the Father were one (John 17:21). When the church is divided, the message becomes diluted. Instead of focusing on majors, the church begins to focus on minors: "Who's in charge?" "What makes a baptism legitimate?" "What prayers can be said?" Or "What songs can be sung?"

When the apostle John wrote the Revelation of Jesus Christ (the actual title of the book of Revelation), he recorded the words of Jesus given to seven churches: Ephesus, Smyrna, Pergamum, Thyatira, Sardis, Philadelphia, and Laodicea. These were diverse churches, all with different leadership, different spiritual practices, and different challenges.

Jesus gave first a word of commendation and then a word of condemnation. It is interesting when I read these chapters in Revelation that there is no word of condemnation for the church at Smyrna or Philadelphia. It is also interesting to me that there was no word of commendation or praise for the church in Laodicea.

All seven of these diverse congregations were addressed by the inspiration of the Holy Spirit through the apostle John, however, as churches. The Greek word used in the book of Revelation for church is *ekklesia.* In chapter 8 we reviewed the meaning of this word; it is worth repeating. The Greek word *ekklesia* is a compound word meaning both "an assembly" and "to call out" or "called-out ones." To summarize Jesus's teaching in Matthew 16:18, the New Testament church is a body of believers who have been called out from the world by God to live as His people under the authority of Jesus Christ.

Recalling the history of the church has not always been pleasant. There have been great men and women—we often refer to them as saints—who were full of the Holy Spirit, lived their lives with integrity, and often died the deaths of martyrs. Not all of the decisions made by the popes or the various leaders of the Protestant Reformation were correct. These were men who were all far from perfect. Their leadership often led to division, and division and sectarianism have always been ugly and not in keeping with the prayer of Jesus in the Gospel of John, chapter 17.

You are, however, not a mere spectator but are to be part of the Body of Christ. It is a body that operates with Jesus at the head. You are a part of the Body if you have fully embraced the wonder.

A few years ago, I had the opportunity to be on a mission trip with World Vision. As pastors, a group of us were invited to see the amazing work that this organization was doing. During the trip, we had a chance to meet the local leaders, meet some of the people and even get out into the very rural community. The first evening we were the honored guests at their worship service. The customs, songs, traditions, musical instruments and service were completely different than anything we had experienced in the past. At the same time, the people were worshiping God and embracing this wonder that binds us all together. The essential truths of the church were there: It was the unique work of Jesus Christ through his sacrifice for our sin that was the very cornerstone of their belief.

The local missionary was an American. He did not bring this culture to the people, he embraced it in order to bring the gospel to them. He was their shepherd and he was interested more in their spiritual condition than in his traditions and personal preferences of song, of style, and even length of service (did I mention the two and a half hour service?).

Yes, you are more than a spectator, you are to be a part of the Body. As a member, you contribute through your prayers, your personal as well as your corporate worship experiences. Your own study of the Word of God brings truth and wisdom to a church, and a world, that needs to not only come together as one, but also needs revival.

Coming together as one, the Body of Christ will bring revival. The differences exemplified in our local churches and denominations are merely examples of the diversity of traditions and practices, but all are part of the one church.

Embrace the wonder!

Endnotes

1. "Summary of Key Findings," *Statistics on Religion in America Report* (n.p., n.d.), web, November 2, 2014.

2. Gal. 3:28.

3. Susan Henderson McHenry, *Therapy with God: Wonderful Counselor, Comforter, Friend* (Xulon, 2008), 25.

4. Dr. Martin Luther, The Large Catechism, trans. F. Bente and W. H. T. Dau, April 1999 [Etext #1722].

5. CBS News, "Bullying: Words Can Kill," September 23, 2013, http://www.cbsnews.com/news/bullying-words-can-kill/

6. Acts 11:26.

7. Heb. 4:12, New Living Translation (NLT).

8. Richard Allen Greene, CNN News, "Christianity goes global as world's largest religion," December 19, 2011.

9. Philip Jenkins, *The Next Christendom: The Coming of Global Christianity* (Future of Christianity Trilogy) (Oxford University Press), 2011.

10. Hugh Henry, "Agios O Theos," in *The Catholic Encyclopedia* (New York: Robert Appleton Company, 1907), retrieved October 19, 2014, from New Advent, www.newadvent.org/cathen/01211b.htm.

11. "Roman Emperors—DIR Irene (Wife of Leo IV)," *Roman Emperors—DIR Irene (Wife of Leo IV)* (n.p., n.d.), web, November 3, 2014.

12. E. Myers, Hosius of Cordova, in *The Catholic Encyclopedia* (New York: Robert Appleton Company, 1910), retrieved October 20, 2014 from New Advent, www.newadvent.org/cathen/07475a.htm.

13. Theodore Noethen, "A Compendium of the History of the Catholic Church: From the Commencement of the Christian Era, to the Ecumenical Council of the Vatican University of California Libraries," January 1, 1870, 221.

14. Achim Nkosi Maseko, *Church Schism and Corruption*, 1st Edition ed. (n.p.: Achim Nkosi Maseko, 2010), 41. Standard.

15. Philip Schaff, "Gregory of Nyssa: Dogmatic Treatises" (New York: Christian Literature, 1892).

16. The Book of Common Prayer (1928), published by the Protestant Episcopal Church in the United States of America, from the web, http://justus.anglican.org/resources/bcp/1928/BCP_1928.htm.

17. Frederick Colman, "A Look at Christianity" (2011), 144, accessed at Xlibris.com.au.

18. Ibid.

19. John Painter, "Just James: The Brother of Jesus in History and Tradition" (Columbia: University of South Carolina Press, 2004), 296.

20. Ibid., 111.

21. William Webster, *The Church of Rome at the bar of history* (Edinburgh: Banner of Truth Trust, 1995), 82–83.

22. "Ineffabilis Deus." *Catholic Library: (1854)* (n.p., n.d.), web, November 3, 2014.

23. "Munificentissimus Deus Defining the Dogma of the Assumption," Apostolic Constitution of Pope Pius XII, November 1, 1950.

24. H. Thurston and A. Shipman, the Rosary, in *The Catholic Encyclopedia* (New York: Robert Appleton Co., 1912), retrieved October 30, 2014, from New Advent, http://www.newadvent.org/cathen/13184b.htm.

25. Bill Bright, *Discover the Book God Wrote* (Wheaton, IL: Tyndale House, 2004), 31.

26. Flavius Josephus, G. A. Williamson, and E. Mary Smallwood, *The Jewish War* (Harmondsworth, Middlesex, England: Penguin, 1981).

27. "An Index of Catholicism's Decline," *WND* (n.p., n.d.), web, October 30, 2014.

28. "Bull of the Crusade," *Catholic Encyclopedia* (n.p., n.d.), web, April 14, 2014.

29. "Johann Tetzel," *Catholic Encyclopedia* (n.p.), http://www.newadvent.org/cathen/14539a.htm, web, November 4, 2014.

30. "The Hope of Salvation for Infants Who Die Without Being Baptised." http://www.vatican.va/roman_curia/ congregations/cfaith/cti_documents/rc_con_cfaith_doc_20070419_un-baptised-infants_en.html (n.d.), web, October 30, 2014.

31. Joseph Cardinal Ratzinger (Pope Benedict XVI), *The Ratzinger Report, An Exclusive Interview on the State of the Church* (San Francisco, CA: Ignatius Press, 1985), 146.

32. "Center for Sex Offender Management—CSOM." *Center for Sex Offender Management—CSOM* (n.p., n.d.), web, October 30, 2014.

33. *US News.* US News & World Report (n.d.), web, October 28, 2014.

34. Catholic University of America, http://faculty.cua.edu/ pennington/Canon%20Law/ElviraCanons.htm.

35. Jeremy Taylor, Charles Page Eden, Reginald Heber, and Alexander Taylor, The Whole Works of the Right Rev. Jeremy Taylor …: Episcopacy (Ulan Press, 2011), 405.

36. NewAdvent, "Catechetical Lecture 23," *Church Fathers: (Cyril of Jerusalem)* (n.p., n.d.), web, December 30, 2014.

37. "Transubstantiation," *Transubstantiation* (n.p., n.d.), web, http:// www.reclaimingeucharistasmeal.com/ transubstantiation.htm, March 15, 2014.

38. David Chidester, "The Symbolism of Learning in St. Augustine," *Harvard Theological Review* 76, 73–90, doi:10.1017/S0017816000018472.

39. "Symbols Are Not Just Symbols." *America Staging* (n.p., n.d.), web, http://americamagazine.org/issue/393/ article/symbols-are-not-just-symbols, February 2, 2014.

40. "Nicene and Ante-Nicene Fathers, Ser. II, Vol. VII: The Catechetical Lectures of S. Cyril: Eucharistic Rites, Liturgy," Nicene and Post-Nicene Fathers, Ser. II, Vol. VII: The Catechetical Lectures of S. Cyril: Eucharistic Rites, Liturgy, accessed December 31, 2014, http://st-takla. org/books/en/ecf/207/2070009.html.

41. "The Council of Trent, the Twenty-Second Session," *The Canons and Decrees of the Sacred and Ecumenical Council of Trent,* ed. and trans. J. Waterworth (London: Dolman, 1848), 152–70.

42. Questions on the Sacrifice of the Mass #357, What is the Mass?, web, October 30, 2014, https://www.ewtn.com/faith/teachings/euchb1a. htm.

43. Fr. Charles, "Learning to Serve: A Guide for New Altar Boys" (Fort Collins, CO: Roman Catholic Books).

44. Nicene Creed.

45. "The Lutheran Reformation," *The History Doctor*, ed. Dr. Larry E. Gates Jr., web, October 30, 2014, http://www.historydoctor.net/ Advanced%20Placement% 20European%20History/Notes/lutheran_ reformation.htm.

46. "William Tyndale," *William Tyndale* (n.p.), http://www.greatsite. com/timeline-english-bible-history/william-tyndale.html, web, May 29, 2014.

47. Nicene Creed, AD 325.

48. Philip Hughes, History of the Church: Volume 2: The Church in the World the Church Created, 244–245, "The Schism of Cerularius."

49. J. M. Hussey, "The Orthodox Church in the Byzantine Empire," *Holytrinitymission*, Clarendon Press Oxford (n.d.), web, December 30, 2014.

50. Michael Cerularius at the Origins of the Byzantine Greek Schism (1054). The Patriarch Michael Cerularius: *"A Formal Schism in 1054 A.D.? What Really Happened?"* James Likoudis, "Social Justice Review," July–August 2010.

51. "Jewish History," *Jewish History*, http://www.jewish history.org/the-black-death/Web. June 29, 2014.

52. William Langland's Piers Plowman: The C Version: a Verse Translation, (Philadelphia: University of Pennsylvania Press, 1996), 100.

53. William Byron Forbush, ed., "Foxes Book of Martyrs."

54. Robert Blair Kaiser, *Inside the Jesuits: How Pope Francis Is Changing the Church and the World* (Lanham: Rowman and Littlefield, 2014).

55. Luke 18:22.

56. Kaiser, *Inside the Jesuits*.

57. "Creative Minority Report: Catholic Reform vs. Protestant Reform," http://www.creativeminorityreport.com/2010/ 06 /catholic-reform-vs-protestant-reform.html, web, November 11, 2014.

58. Bruce L. Shelley, *Church History in Plain Language* (Nashville, TN: Thomas Nelson, 2008), 233.

59. Augnet, Your reference site to St. Augustine of Hippo and the Order of St. Augustine, copyright 2010, "*Home* (n.p.), http://augnet. org/default.asp?ipageid=2210, web, November 2, 2014.

60. Augnet.

61. Richard P. Bucher, *The Ecumenical Luther: The Development and Use of His Doctrinal Hermeneutic.* (St. Louis: Concordia, 2003). Print.

62. Ibid.

63. Carl Becker, *Like Christ by Grace: Pursuing the Prize of Christlikeness by God's Grace.* S.l.: West Bow Pr, 2012. Print. P. 152.

64. "Pope Paul III," *Catholic Encyclopedia* (n.p.), http://www.newadvent.org/cathen/11579a.htm, web, November 2, 2014.

65. The major theme of my writing has been that we are one church and that theological disagreements are, for the most part, unhelpful. I'm not talking about apostasies like Gnosticism, which taught that salvation was achieved by some hidden knowledge, or Arianism, which taught that Jesus was a created being and was condemned by the Council at Nicaea.

Extended Bibliography

Bingham, D. J. *Pocket History of the Church*. Downers Grove, IL: InterVarsity Press, 2002.

Rhodes, Ron. *Reasoning from the Scriptures with Catholics*. Eugene, OR: Harvest House, 2000.

Ashe, Geoffrey. *The Virgin*. London: Routledge & Paul, 1976.

Christman, Bill. *Forgiving the Catholic Church*, Enumclaw, WA: Winepress, 2012.

Guy, Laurie. *Introducing Early Christianity: A Topical Survey of Its Life, Beliefs, and Practices*. Downers Grove, IL: InterVarsity Press, 2004.

Jenkins, Philip. *The Next Christendom: The Coming of Global Christianity*. Oxford, NY: Oxford University Press, 2011.

McCarthy, James G. *The Gospel According to Rome*. Eugene, OR: Harvest House, 1995.

Christian History Time Line: 200 Fascinating Events in Church History. Torrance, CA: Rose, 1998.

Jenkins, Philip. *The New Faces of Christianity: Believing the Bible in the Global Douth*. Oxford, NY: Oxford University Press, 2006.

Geisler, Norman L., and Ralph E. MacKenzie. *Roman Catholics and Evangelicals: Agreements and Differences*. Grand Rapids, MI: Baker Books, 1995.

Grudem, Wayne A. *Systematic Theology: An Introduction to Biblical Doctrine.* Leicester, England; Grand Rapids, MI: InterVarsity Press, Zondervan, 1994.

Boettner, Loraine. *Roman Catholicism.* Phillipsburg, NJ: Presbyterian and Reformed Publishing, 1983.

Curtis, A. K., J. S. Lang, and Randy Petersen. *The 100 Most Important Events in Christian History.* Grand Rapids, MI: F. H. Revell, 1998.

Hart, David B. *The Story of Christianity: An Illustrated History of 2000 Years of the Christian Faith.* London: Quercus, 2011.

Fahlbusch, Erwin, and Geoffrey W. Bromiley. *The Encyclopedia of Christianity.* Grand Rapids, MI; Leiden, Netherlands: Wm. B. Eerdmans Brill, 1999.

Martin, James C., John A. Beck, and David G. Hansen. *A Visual Guide to Bible Events: Fascinating Insights into Where They Happened and Why.* Grand Rapids, MI: Baker Books, 2009.

Martin, James C., John A. Beck, and David G. Hansen. *A Visual Guide to Gospel Events: Fascinating Insights into Where They Happened and Why.* Grand Rapids, MI: Baker Books, 2010.

Collins, Michael, and Matthew A. Price. *The Story of Christianity.* New York: DK, 1999.

Morgan, Robert J. *On This Day in Christian History: 365 Amazing and Inspiring Stories about Saints, Martyrs, and Heroes.* Nashville, TN: Thomas Nelson, 2010.

Olson, Roger E. *The Story of Christian Theology: Twenty Centuries of Tradition & Reform.* Downers Grove, IL: InterVarsity Press, 1999.

Extended Bibliography

Shelley, Bruce L. *Church History in Plain Language.* Nashville, TN: Thomas Nelson, 2008.

Sproul, R. C. *Are We Together? A Protestant Analyzes Roman Catholicism.* Orlando, FL: Reformation Trust, 2012.

Watkins, James A. *Jesus in the World: The First 600 Years.* CreateSpace Independent Publishing Platform, 2014.

Stark, Rodney. *The Rise of Christianity: How the Obscure, Marginal Jesus Movement Became the Dominant Religious Force in the Western World in a Few Centuries.* San Francisco: HarperSanFrancisco, 1997.

Stevenson, Kenneth, and Gary R. Habermas. *Verdict on the Shroud: Evidence for the Death and Resurrection of Jesus Christ.* Ann Arbor, MI: Servant Books, 1981.

Webster, William. *The Church of Rome at the Bar of History.* Edinburgh: Banner of Truth Trust, 1995.

White, James A. *The Roman Catholic Controversy.* Minneapolis, MN: Bethany House, 1996.

Hahn, Scott, and Kimberly Hahn. *Rome Sweet Home: Our Journey to Catholicism.* San Francisco: Ignatius Press, 1993.

McHenry, Susan Henderson. *Therapy with God: Wonderful Counselor, Comforter, Friend.* Xulon, 2008.

Glossary of Terms

Apocrypha

The Apocrypha, also called the deuterocanonical books, are those ancient, Old Testament type books that were not part of the Hebrew Bible. They are considered canon, from the Greek word for "straight," and are included in the Bible by the Roman Catholic and most Eastern or Orthodox Churches but not by the Protestant Church. The Old Testament books in this category include Judith, the Wisdom of Solomon, Tobit, Sirach (Ecclesiasticus), Baruch, and 1 and 2 Maccabees. Most scholars agree that these books do not have the same historical usage as the rest of the Old Testament and have limited theological importance.

Assumption of Mary

The Roman Catholic Church teaches that Mary never died but was carried away into heaven. This is one of the most recent official dogmas related to Mary and is related to the Immaculate Conception. Early church history recorded that Mary died in Ephesus at age sixty-four; later the records stated her body was subsequently resurrected or taken to heaven. The pope officially defined the doctrine of the Assumption of Mary by in 1950.

Baby Dedication

An acknowledgment that parents and the church have a very important role in both the physical and spiritual development of the child. It is not considered a sacrament, but is celebrated in many non-Catholic churches. It is not recognized as a separate event in the Catholic Church, which baptizes infants.

Baptism

The Roman Catholic Church baptizes infants, typically within a few weeks of birth. In the Catholic Church, baptism provides remission of sin, both original and actual; it provides the Holy Spirit, regenerating the soul of the infant. Protestant Churches that baptize infants often consider it a symbol of the New Covenant, similar to the ancient rite of circumcision, or both. Evangelicals typically follow the teaching of Believers Baptism and baptize individuals after they are able to confess their belief in Jesus. The early Church initially baptized adults as an initiation into the Church and typically considered that baptism forgave sin.

Bible

Consists of both an Old Testament and a New Testament. The Catholic Old Testament includes seven more books than the Jewish Bible. For Roman Catholics these deuterocanonical books, meaning second canon, of the Old Testament are Judith, the Wisdom of Solomon, 1 and 2 Esdras, Tobit, Sirach (Ecclesiasticus), the Epistle of Jeremiah, Baruch, 1 and 2 Maccabees, and certain additions to the Jewish books of Esther and Daniel. The Catholics would view the Bible and tradition as equal in determining doctrine and religious rites.

The Protestant Reformation elevated the status of the Bible over tradition. The additional books (above) were not included in later editions of Protestant Bibles. There is no difference in the New Testaments in Catholic and Protestant Bibles.

Catholic

The term is derived from a Greek word meaning "universal." It was first widely applied to the church after the Nicene Creed defined a belief in "one holy, catholic, and apostolic church." It was the name formally given to the church by the Roman emperor. It is not exclusively the name of the Roman Catholic Church, as the Orthodox Church could easily claim to be the recipient of this particular reference, as they claim the Roman or Latin Rite broke communion with the rest of the church in AD 1054. The Roman Catholic Church is the largest of twenty-three recognized Catholic Churches, and in this capacity is officially known as the Latin Church. With more than one billion members, it is headquartered in Vatican City. The Eastern or various Orthodox Churches (the other twenty-two) also use the word *catholic*. In reality all Churches that can embrace the Nicene Creed may consider themselves part of the "one holy, catholic, and apostolic church."

Celibacy of the Clergy

The Roman Catholic Church defines celibacy as the renunciation of marriage. An encyclical of Pope Paul VI in 1968 affirmed the celibacy of the priest (first documented at the Synod of Elvira in Spain in AD 306), banning marriages and concubines for priests. The history of celibacy in the church is marked with great controversy, which continues to this day. Most of the apostles were married; Peter was married, and seven popes were married. It was likely the teachings of Gnosticism that material things and sexual relations even in marriage were evil that led to teachings on celibacy. However, clergy remained married without any restrictions until the sixth century.

Church, Institution

The Roman Catholic Church clearly identifies the Church as an institution: "The church, as has been seen, is a society formed of living men, not a mere mystical union of souls. As such it resembles other societies. Like them, it has its code of rules, its executive officers, its ceremonial observances" (Source: *New Advent/Catholic Encyclopedia*). Protestant theology defines *church* through the meaning of the Greek word *ekklesia*. This is a compound word formed from two Greek words meaning "an assembly" and "to call out" or "called-out ones." In essence neither a building nor a denomination, the Church is the body of believers who have been called out from the world by God to live as His people under the authority of Jesus Christ.

Church, Structure

There are various different organizational structures in the different denominations.

Many, including the Roman Catholic, follow an episcopal form of governance, from the Greek word *Episkopos*, sometimes translated as "overseer" or "bishop." All Catholics, clergy and laity, submit to the leadership of the pope, considered to be the successor of Peter and the Vicar of Christ. Non–Roman Catholics would object to the pope as being a successor of Peter and consider Christ to be the ultimate and actual head of the church.

Communion

In the Roman Catholic Church, Communion is called the Eucharist, defined as a sacrament that spiritually reenacts the crucifixion of Jesus Christ in a non-bloody manner. The Catholic belief is that Christ is present in the Eucharist fully through the transformation of the elements into the body and blood of Christ. In other Churches Communion is a sacrament that may also embrace the presence of Christ in some form, either in the elements or within the community. In some congregations Communion, while a sacrament and very special, is strictly a memorial service. (See also First Communion.)

Confirmation

A sacrament of the Roman Catholic Church that dates back to the fourth century. Confirmation is typically received in later adolescence or the teenage years. The Catholic Church considers it the second of the three sacraments of initiation (baptism being the first and Communion the third). Confirmation is regarded as the perfection of baptism, where the candidate affirms the baptismal vows typically recited when he or she was an infant by the parent or godparent. Confirmation became important in the Church when baptism became something administered to an infant rather than an adult, and Confirmation assumed the rite of the initiation.

Converting/Conversion   The Roman Catholic Church would consider anyone joining its church, typically by being baptized, as converting to Catholicism and anyone who leaves and joins another church as converting to a different/false religion. Conversion for a non-Catholic is considered to happen when a person embraces Jesus and Christianity and is not directly tied to membership in a particular Church or denomination.

Denominations   The Roman Catholic Church officially views all other Christian denominations as fallen away. *Extra ecclesiam nulla salus* is a dogma of the Roman Catholic Church and can literally be translated as "outside of the church, there is no salvation." Because this was a widely distributed doctrine declared *ex cathedra*, it is difficult to modify. However, recently Pope Francis said, "The Lord has redeemed all of us, all of us, with the Blood of Christ: all of us, not just Catholics. Everyone." The first denominational split in the church was in

AD 1054, when the East (Greek Orthodox) and the West (Latin Rite) separated. Later denominations came into existence in Western Europe when the Reformation was successful. Recently nondenominational churches have been on the rise, focusing on the major tenets of the faith.

First Communion

In the Roman Catholic Church, children, typically around seven or eight years old, take classes on the meaning and the sacrament of Holy Communion (Holy Eucharist). This is an important event in the life of a Catholic, as the participation in the Eucharist is the central part of Catholic worship. In the early Church, Communion underwent a number of theological and social changes. In the early apostolic era, Communion was considered to be a part of a common meal called an Agape feast. The anti-Nicene Church continued to practice the Agape or love feast. However, with the Edict of Milan, which ended the Roman persecution of the Church, and the official endorsement of the Church as the state church of Rome, the entire worship service became the liturgy and Communion the central part, which was officiated by the priest.

Hell

Hell is considered the state of being separated from God for eternity. Typically Christians will identify those who have been rejected by God or choose to not accept

God's merciful love as assigned to a place
called hell. Hell is the place created by God
for the punishment of the evil and fallen
angels (Matthew 25:41) and those whose
names are not written in the book of life
(Revelation 20:15). It is the final destiny of
every person who does not receive salvation,
where he or she will be punished for his or
her sins. People will be consigned to hell
after the last judgment.

Icons

Both the East and the West went through
periods when religious images were used for
a while but then later destroyed by those who
wanted to purify the Church in their attempt
to honor the Second Commandment. In the
East very clever artists solved the problem by
creating icons that were not carved or graven
but flat, two-dimensional representations or
likeness of events (parables, the crucifixion)
as well as Jesus Christ, the Virgin Mary,
angels, and the saints.

Immaculate Conception

A Roman Catholic teaching that was not
officially defined until 1854 that Mary, as
the mother of Christ, was conceived without
original sin. The Bible teaches that all have
sinned, and the Immaculate Conception
does not mean that Mary never sinned;
however, many Roman Catholics assume this
is the meaning of the doctrine.

Latin

Latin became the official language of the
Church with Jerome's translation of the

Bible into Latin, or the Latin Vulgate. Latin became not only the primary but the only authorized translation of the Holy Scripture and the official language of the Mass. For more than 1,700 years, the Western (Roman Catholic) Church used exclusively Latin. The Second Vatican Council in 1965 permitted the Mass to be celebrated in the language of the people. In the Middle Ages the Latin language evolved quickly into numerous dialects, and since the Bible and all liturgical prayers and ecclesiastical and theological discourses were in classical Latin, only the few who were well educated and primarily the clergy were able to read and understand it. By the Middle Ages, many of the rural parish priests could read the letters and pronounce the words but were unable to understand fully what they read. Translating the Bible into the common language of the people was greatly contested by the Catholic Church, and many were persecuted as a result.

Infallibility of the Pope   The teaching that in matters of religious doctrine and faith, the proclamations by the pope are to be considered infallible. The teaching was made official in 1870, and the logic behind it is that the bishop of Rome (the pope) is the direct successor of Peter, who was given the keys to the kingdom. Protestants will point to the lack of evidence that Peter was ever a pope, the lack of any mention of succession or infallibility in the

Bible, and numerous decisions and doctrines of the Roman Catholic Church endorsed by various popes that had been reversed over the years.

Limbo

A place for infants who die before being baptized and for Old Testament saints. There is no official Roman Catholic Church doctrine on the eternal state of babies. However, most Catholic teachers typically affirm the theory of limbo based on the strong tradition and personal opinions. These unofficial teachings regarding limbo have not been discouraged. There is no indication in the scriptures of a need for a place for infants or for others who have died without the benefit of baptism. Contemporary pastors and theologians typically would point to the mercy and wisdom of God regarding their eternal state. The word *limbo* was first used to describe the temporary state of the dead Jewish faithful until the time of Christ (i.e., Abraham's Bosom).

Liturgy

The Catholic Church is both liturgical as well as sacramental in public worship. This means the order of service is determined based on particular liturgies that the hierarchy has approved. The Roman Catholic liturgy has four sections, starting with some introductory rites, followed by the liturgy of the Word, the liturgy of the Eucharist, and some concluding rites. Many non-Catholic denominations are also liturgical in their worship and sacraments.

Mass (see also *liturgy*)   In the Roman Catholic Church, the Mass is synonymous with their Eucharist (Lord's Supper/Communion). It is thought to be handed down directly from the apostles and is officially known as the Sacrifice of the Mass where Christ, through the ministry of the priest, is sacrificed in an unbloody manner under the appearance of bread and wine. This offering, combined with partaking of the Eucharist, fulfills a Catholic's obligation to be present weekly, traditionally on Sunday but now often as well Saturday night. Mass is actually a Latin term that refers to dismissal prior to the central and most holy part of the early Christian liturgy. At this dismissal the catechumens (people preparing to be accepted into Christianity) were released, and the remaining faithful received Communion together.

Penance/Confession   Penance (Confession) was introduced in the Church over a number of centuries. We have writings from the early fourth century that show that the bishop encouraged penitents to wear sackcloth, sit in ashes, and shave their heads. The Council of Toledo (AD 589) prescribed the sacrament of penance to be unrepeatable. As a result penance was considered an once-in-a-lifetime opportunity and typically was not received until very late in life. However, in the thirteenth century,

the Fourth Lateran Council required that
the sacrament of penance be individually
received annually. In the Protestant
churches, confession is good for the soul,
but the power of a priest to forgive sins
uniquely typically is not taught.

Peter as First Pope

The Roman Catholic Church teaches that
Jesus Christ appointed St. Peter as the head
of the Church. Further, this teaching is
illustrated on the Day of Pentecost, when
Peter addressed the crowd, and three
thousand were converted to Christianity.
The teaching continued that Peter led
the early Church, founded the Church in
Rome, and named his successor to continue
this tradition. The lineage of popes is
documented by Rome, with Pope Francis
identified as the 266th pope. There are
historical problems with this teaching: Peter
was certainly a strong leader of the early
Church, but the early Church in Jerusalem
chose James, the brother of Jesus, to be the
first bishop (per the writings of Eusebius,
official biographer of Constantine and St.
Clement in the third century). Peter likely
made it to Rome and was likely martyred,
as tradition tells us; however, he and other
early bishops of Rome didn't take the title of
pope or *pontific maximus* until three to four
centuries later. The early Church, until the
eleventh century, was ruled by five patriarchs
(bishops) in the key cities of Jerusalem,
Antioch, Alexandria, Constantinople, and

Rome. The bishop of Rome's insistence on being the head of the church led to the first split between East and West in AD 1054.

Prayer to Saints

In Roman Catholicism saints (departed holy Christians) and angels will make intercessions on behalf of individuals still on Earth. In this way requests can be made to saints and the Virgin Mary to pray for us. Saints and the Virgin Mary are not to be worshipped, though the veneration of the Virgin Mary is an encouraged and important practice for most Roman Catholics. Reformers of the sixteenth century declared that the veneration and honor of the Virgin Mary and saints all too quickly, and too often, took the form of worship that was reserved for God alone.

Priesthood

Roman Catholicism teaches that the Catholic priest is the minister of divine worship and especially of the highest act of worship, the sacrifice. "Every religion has its priests, exercising more or less exalted sacerdotal functions as intermediaries between man and the Divinity. The Priesthood includes the bishop who is both a priest and a high priest; he has chief control of the Divine worship. He has the fullness of the priesthood, and administers all the sacraments" (source: *New Advent/Catholic Encyclopedia*). The early Apostolic Church did not have a priesthood but did have bishops (a translation of the Greek word

presbuterion) and deacons. The priesthood in
the Church didn't appear until much later
and is thought to have both Old Testament
and pagan origins.

Purgatory

Purgatory (Latin *purgare*, "to make clean,
to purify"), in accordance with Catholic
teaching, is a place or condition of temporal
punishment for those who, departing this
life in God's grace, are not entirely free from
venial faults (sins) or have not fully paid
the satisfaction due to their transgressions
(source: *New Advent/Catholic Encyclopedia*).
Purgatory is not so much a place (i.e.,
neither heaven nor hell) but a transition
where sinners must first endure a state of
purification. The teachings of purgatory
emerged in the Middle Ages and changed
greatly because of the Reformation.
The Reformers of the sixteenth century
rejected purgatory, as it was not taught in
scripture and was thought to be contrary
to the teachings of salvation, grace, and
sanctification.

Role of Clergy

In the Roman Catholic Church, clergy are
special ordained men who have the power
to minister officially in the priesthood as
well as the power to offer the sacrifice and
dispense the sacraments. The Reformation
of the sixteenth century typically embraced
the priesthood of all believers and denied
that ordained clergy had any particular

sacerdotal function that was unique. However, they fulfilled a customary and necessary leadership role.

Role of the Church   The Roman Catholic Church identifies the Church as a living society of priests, executives, and other leaders who have unique and spiritual roles in filling an intermediary position between God and man. The Reformation was typically critical in both the role of the priest and the power and authority of the Church.

Reformation   The culmination of a religious revival that was most obviously successful when Martin Luther nailed his Ninety-Five Theses on the church door in 1517. A combination of political, economic, and spiritual opportunities resulted in the first successful challenge to the role and the absolute authority of the Roman pontiff. As a result nearly half of the population of Europe decided to follow various divergent churches. These churches were often organized along geographical or national borders until religious freedom became a cornerstone of unalienable rights of the people (e.g., America).

Rosary   Millions of Catholics use the rosary, and its introduction is often attributed to St. Dominick. According to many accounts, St. Dominick had an apparition of the

Virgin Mary, who was said to have spoken to him and told him the key to his success in ministry would be to teach the people how to say the rosary. The rosary helps the person who is praying count the prayers and the sequence of prayers, with certain beads being different sizes or spaced differently, acknowledging either the end of a decade (ten prayers) or the beginning of a different type of prayer. According to many Protestants and detractors of the rosary, it encourages both vain repetitions in prayer as well as prayers directed to the Virgin Mary, a practice the Reformers in the sixteenth century discouraged.

Sacraments

Churches embrace the sacraments as either the means of grace, as in the Roman Catholic Church, or the symbols of grace, as defined in most non-Catholic Churches. History records that the early Church practiced three sacraments: baptism, the Agape feast, and the Eucharist. The Roman Catholic Church acknowledges seven sacraments:

- Baptism (as infants or adults)
- Eucharist (the Lord's Supper or Communion)
- Reconciliation (Penance or Confession)
- Confirmation
- Marriage
- Holy Orders
- Anointing of the Sick (Extreme Unction or Last Rites)

The number of sacraments in other
churches ranges from as few as two to as
many as thirteen, possibly more.

Saints

The word *saint* comes from the Greek
hágios, which means "separated" or
"consecrated to God." In the New
Testament, the word is used more than sixty
times and always is in reference to living
Christians who are impacting the world.
Scripturally speaking saints are the body
of Christ. In the twelfth century, a papal
bull confirmed the process of canonizing
a saint to include the inquiries into his or
her life and whether miracles are attributed
to him or her. The Church has canonized
more than ten thousand named saints,
the vast majority of them within the past
one hundred years. The Catholic Church
doesn't officially endorse praying to the
saints but supports "asking our departed
brothers and sisters in Christ, the saints,
for their intercession" (source: *New Advent/
Catholic Encyclopedia*).

Salvation

For the Roman Catholic, salvation is thought
to be available through holding to the
teachings of the Catholic faith. Typically
the common thought is that there are
many ways to lose salvation but no ways to
be completely sure of it. In contrast most
Protestant Churches teach assurance of
salvation through the grace of God. There
are many debates, however, related to

whether it is possible for a person to lose his
or her salvation.

Sign of the Cross

The early Church started embracing a small
sign of a cross, typically on foreheads, to
represent both the cross of Jesus and the
belief in the Trinity: the Father, Son, and
Holy Ghost. The early-fifth-century records
show how a bishop would complete a
blessing, with three fingers and forming a
cross. The use of two fingers and the sign
of the cross used in the Roman Catholic
Church today can be traced to the ninth
century and Pope Leo IV. Interestingly the
Western or Roman Catholic Church uses
two fingers (symbolizing the dual nature of
Christ, divine and human) and left shoulder
to right whereas the Eastern or Orthodox
Church uses three fingers, symbolizing the
Trinity, and movement from right shoulder
to left.

Statues, Venerating

Statues and images of Jesus, Mary, and
individual saints are commonly found in
both Catholic sacred spaces and residences.
However, Catholics are expected to venerate
the persons represented by the statues,
not the statues themselves. Initially the
church followed the Jewish tradition of
never representing God through a graven
image. To the early church, that meant
Jesus Christ as well, so they did not erect
statues of saints or place figures of Jesus

on the cross. Statues and crucifixes as we know them today were later additions to Christian worship and typically are attributed to the early Renaissance period. The Eastern or Orthodox Church embraced icons as early as the third century that were carefully designed to be flat and not three dimensional, therefore not graven images. At times people aggressively opposed their use, and the church sent troops against those who used them. This movement, called iconoclasm, was finally reconciled in the ninth century.

Tabernacle

The tabernacle of the Old Testament is replicated in the Roman Catholic Church. The word means "dwelling place," and just as God dwelt within the tabernacle in the wilderness as well as in the Temple of Solomon, Roman Catholics believe that in the consecrated host (i.e., bread), Jesus is present and dwells in the locked, typically golden tabernacle placed toward the back of the sanctuary. As a result people will genuflect or kneel before the tabernacle, and the consecrated host displayed in a golden stand called a monstrance, sometimes called an ostensorium, may be worshiped, as the Roman Catholic Church teaches it is God. Protestants typically reject the remaining presence of Christ in the elements of bread or wine and would not consider worship of the elements to be appropriate.

**Virgin Mary,
Assumption of the**

The assumption of Mary is a Roman Catholic belief, one of the four Marian dogmas that was formally adopted in the twentieth century, that the Virgin Mary, having completed the course of her earthly life, was assumed body and soul into heavenly glory. Pope Pius XII dogmatically and infallibly defined this doctrine on November 1, 1950. Mary is also referred to as the queen of heaven, a term that finds its history in the fifth century and from the Council of Ephesus pronouncement that Mary was Theotokos, or Mother of God. While there was little documentation of Mary's life in the early Church, she was believed to have died in Ephesus. Early writings circulated during the fifth century, the *Transitus Baetae Mariae*, spoke of her supremacy and her being attended by virgins and angels. This book was condemned by the early Church as heresy in 495 AD, by Pope Gelasius. During the same time, the church openly debated the question of whether Mary should be referred to as the Mother of God or Mother of the Messiah primarily because of the belief that Jesus, as God the Son, existed as the logos from eternity as God.

**Virgin Mary,
Perpetual Virginity**

The church universally teaches that Jesus was born of a virgin. However, there are other teachings related to Mary that are not universally embraced. The Roman Catholic Church teaches that Mary was a perpetual virgin despite being married to Joseph.

210

Further, it dismisses biblical mentions of Jesus's having brothers and sisters as referring to cousins. Other related teachings in the Roman Catholic Church include that Mary has been named the co-redeemer with Jesus and the queen of heaven. Many scholars claim that the teaching that Mary remained a perpetual virgin contradicts the Bible and is contrary to everything we know about what would be normative at that time in history (i.e., women did not become engaged or married to remain virgins).